THEMATIC UNIT

African Americans

Written by Donna Evert

D1278392

Teacher Created Materials, Inc.
P.O. Box 1040
Huntington Beach, CA 92647
©1995 Teacher Created Materials, Inc.
Made in U.S.A.

ISBN-1-55734-590-2

Edited by
Janet Cain

Illustrated by
Agnes S. Palinay

Cover Art by
Blanca Apodaca LaBounty

Table of Contents

Introduction 3

The Talking Eggs by Robert D. San Souci (Dial Books, 1989) 5
   (Available from Penguin Books: Canada & Australia / Bodley Head: UK)
   Summary—Sample Plan—Overview of Activities—Sequencing—Polar Opposites—Folk Tale
   Comparison Chart—"Eggsamining" Weights—Story Pyramid—Cause and Effect—Egg Art

Roll of Thunder, Hear My Cry by Mildred Taylor (Penguin Books, 1991) 15
   (Available from Penguin Books: Canada, UK, & Australia)
   Summary—Sample Plan—Overview and Activities—Vocabulary and Activities—Journal and
   Discussion Questions—Story Map—Polar Opposites—Character Map—Similes—Balanced or
   Biased?—Classification—Take a Walk in Cassie's Shoes—Cassie and You

One More River to Cross by Jim Haskins (Scholastic, 1992) 28
   (Available from Scholastic: Canada & UK / Ashton Scholastic Pty. Ltd.: Australia)
   Summary—Sample Plan—Overview of Activities—Understanding Discrimination—Madam C.J.
   Walker: A Success Story—Matthew Henson Explored the North Pole—Eleanor Roosevelt Helped
   Marian Anderson—Ralph Bunche and the Meaning of Peace—Charles Drew and the Study of
   Blood—Shirley Chisholm as a Member of Congress—An Award for Ronald McNair—Timeline—
   Hero Comparison Chart—Career Survey

Across the Curriculum 42
   Language Arts: Daily Writing Activities—Poetry (Clerihew—Diamonte—Couplet—
                        Limerick—List Poem—Acrostic—Alliteration)—Word Search—Super
                        Box Dance—Future Wheel—Paideia
   Math: Mankala—Using a Grid—Nsikwi
   Science: "Eggsperiments"—Build an Insulator—Make a Compass
   Social Studies: Venn Diagram—Comparing Maps—Concentration—Kwanzaa
   Art: Story Filmstrips
   Theater Arts: Present a Puppet Show—Present a Skit
   Life Skills: African Recipes

Culminating Activities 72
   Cultures Day—Heritage Quilt—Mural

Unit Management 75
   Bulletin Boards—Research Center

Bibliography 77

Answer Key 79

Introduction

African Americans contains a comprehensive whole-language, thematic unit. Its 80 reproducible pages are filled with a wide variety of lesson ideas designed for use with intermediate and junior high school students. At its core are three high-quality reading selections: *The Talking Eggs; Roll of Thunder, Hear My Cry;* and *One More River to Cross.*

There are activities for each selection which set the stage for reading, encourage the enjoyment of the book, and extend the concepts. Activities are also provided that integrate the curriculum areas of language arts (including writing assignments), math, science, social studies, art, theater arts, and life skills. Many of these activities are conducive to the use of cooperative learning groups.

This unit can be used in its entirety when studying about different cultures, or it can be broken into sections that are relevant to topics being studied, such as segregation in history or folk tales in literature. It is important that the contributions of African Americans be recognized in all areas of the curriculum throughout the year.

This thematic unit includes:

- ☐ **Literature Selections**—summaries of three books with related activities that cross the curriculum

- ☐ **Planning Guides**—suggestions for sequencing lessons for each day of the unit

- ☐ **Overview of Activities**—a brief description of the activities that are related to each book

- ☐ **Curriculum Connections**—relating the theme to language arts, math, science, social studies, art, theater arts, and life skills

- ☐ **Writing Ideas**—writing suggestions and activities that cross the curriculum

- ☐ **Group Projects**—to foster cooperative learning

- ☐ **Hands-On Activities**—providing opportunities for students to be active learners

- ☐ **Bulletin Board Ideas**—time-saving suggestions and plans for bulletin boards

- ☐ **Research Topics**—listing a variety of topics that can be used to extend and enrich learning

- ☐ **Culminating Activities**—which require students to synthesize their learning and participate in activities that can be shared with others

- ☐ **Bibliography**—suggesting additional literature and nonfiction books on the theme

> To keep this valuable resource intact so it can be used year after year, you may wish to punch holes in the pages and store them in a three-ring binder.

Introduction (cont.)

Why Whole Language?

A whole-language approach involves children in using all modes of communication: reading, writing, listening, observing, illustrating, experiencing, and doing. Communication skills are interconnected and integrated into lessons that emphasize the whole of language rather than isolating its parts. The lessons revolve around selected literature. Reading is not taught as a separate subject from writing and spelling, for example. A student reads, writes, speaks, listens, and thinks in response to a literature experience introduced by the teacher. In this way, language skills grow naturally, stimulated by involvement and interest in the topic at hand.

Why Thematic Planning?

One very useful tool for implementing an integrated whole language program is thematic planning. By choosing a theme with correlating literature selections for a unit of study, a teacher can plan activities throughout the day that lead to a cohesive, in-depth study of the topic. Students will be practicing and applying their skills in meaningful contexts. Consequently, they will tend to learn and retain more. Both teachers and students will be freed from a day that is broken into unrelated segments of isolated drill and practice.

Why Cooperative Learning?

Besides academic skills and content, students need to learn social skills. No longer can this area of development be taken for granted. Students must learn to work cooperatively in groups in order to function well in modern society. Group activities should be a regular part of school life, and teachers should consciously include social objectives as well as academic objectives in their planning. The teacher should clarify and monitor the qualities of good group interaction, just as he/she would clarify and monitor the academic goals of the project.

Why Big Books?

An excellent cooperative, whole-language activity is the production of big books. Groups of students or the whole class can apply their language skills, content knowledge, and creativity to produce a big book that can become a part of the classroom library to be read and reread. These books make excellent culminating projects for sharing beyond the classroom with parents, librarians, and others. Big books can be produced in many ways, and this thematic unit book includes directions for some methods you may choose.

The Talking Eggs

by Robert D. San Souci

Summary

This story is an adaptation of a Creole folk tale. It is the story of two sisters who live with their widowed mother. Rose is lazy, cruel, and greedy, just like the mother. In contrast, Blanche is hard-working, kind, and generous. Blanche shows compassion to an old woman by getting her a drink of water at the well. Her mother and sister are angry that Blanche took so long at the well, so they become abusive. Blanche runs away into the woods where she sees the old woman again. The old woman takes Blanche to her cabin. This results in a magical adventure in which Blanche sees many unusual things, including talking eggs. The old woman allows Blanche to take some of the eggs with her. Blanche discovers that the eggs she was allowed to take were plain on the outside but full of valuables on the inside. Rose and the mother are jealous of Blanche's treasures, so Rose goes into the woods in search of the old woman. Rose is greedy and takes the eggs that are fancy on the outside, going against what the old woman told her to do. Rose and her mother find that the beautiful eggs have a variety of horrible creatures inside of them.

The outline below is a suggested plan for using the various activities presented in this section of *African Americans*. Each lesson can take from one to several days to complete. You should adapt these ideas to fit your own classroom situation.

Sample Plan

Lesson 1
- Prepare a bulletin board (page 75).
- Set the stage (page 6).
- Read and discuss *The Talking Eggs*.
- Compare folk tales (page 10).
- Complete an art project (page 14).

Lesson 2
- Complete a daily writing activity (page 42).
- Sequence story events (page 8).
- Write a poem (pages 43–44).
- Make a Venn diagram (page 59).
- Conduct "Eggsperiments" (page 54).
- Conduct a Paideia seminar on *The Talking Eggs* (pages 48–49).

Lesson 3
- Complete a daily writing activity (page 42).
- Make a word search (page 45).
- Determine character traits using polar opposites (page 9).
- Complete an art project (page 14).
- Write a poem (pages 43–44).
- Play Mankala (page 51).
- Prepare a puppet show (page 69).

Lesson 4
- Complete a daily writing activity (page 42).
- Make a graph of average egg weights (page 11).
- Create a story pyramid (page 12).
- Conduct "Eggsperiments" (page 55).
- Write a poem (pages 43–44).

Lesson 5
- Complete a daily writing activity (page 42).
- Complete an art project (page 14).
- Examine cause and effect (page 13).
- Present a skit (page 70).
- Select culminating activities (pages 72–74).

Lesson 6
- Play Nsikwi (page 53).
- Conduct "Eggsperiments" (page 56).
- Produce a story filmstrip (page 68).
- Make an African recipe (page 71).
- Complete culminating activities (pages 72–74).

Overview of Activities

SETTING THE STAGE

1. **Bulletin Board.** Display the "Folk Tales from Around the World" bulletin board (page 75).

2. **Prediction.** Have students predict what the story might be about by hearing the title and looking at the cover illustration.

3. **SSR.** Reserve 15 minutes each day for SSR (sustained, silent reading) of folk tales. See the bibliography (pages 77–78) for the titles of some folk tales.

4. **Egg Related Expressions.** Ask students to brainstorm a list of egg related expressions. Some examples include: "over easy," "sunny side up," "walking on eggs," "smells like a rotten egg," "Don't put all your eggs in one basket," and "Don't count your chickens before they're hatched." Write their suggestions on the chalkboard. Discuss the meaning of each expression.

ENJOYING THE BOOK

1. **Comprehension Activity.** Sequence the most important events of the story using the sequencing worksheet (page 8). Some students may want to cut events out of the worksheet and paste them in order on another sheet of paper and include illustrations.

2. **Polar Opposites.** Students rate the characters and events in the story using a scale of 1 to 5 (page 9). Then they write information from the story that provides evidence to support the rating they have chosen.

3. **"Eggsamining" Weights.** Students begin by stating a hypothesis about the relationship between an egg's size and weight (page 11). Then they weigh three of each type of egg: small, medium, and large or jumbo. After students determine an average for each type of egg, they create a bar graph using the data. Students conclude the activity by determining if the bar graph supports their hypothesis.

4. **Line Graph.** Set up a line graph on the chalkboard. Label the vertical axis with "Number of Eggs" and label the horizontal axis with the names of the days of the week. Take a poll each day to see how many eggs were eaten by your students. Record the data on the graph. At the end of the week, evaluate the results. You can extend this activity by polling several classes and recording the data on the graph using different colors of chalk.

5. **Story Pyramid.** A story pyramid (page 12) is used to organize important information from the story. First, have students study the example of a story pyramid. Then ask them to create their own, using information from the story.

6. **Cause and Effect.** Have students determine cause-and-effect relationships using events in the story (page 13).

7. **Word Search.** Ask students to make a list of twenty words that pertain to the story. Have them create a word search (page 45), using those words. Have students trade papers with a partner and solve each other's word search.

8. **Venn Diagram.** Have students use a Venn diagram to compare and contrast characters in the story (page 59).

9. **Writing Activities.** Assign students a daily writing activity (page 42) or a type of poem (pages 43–44) through which they can express information about the story.

6

Overview of Activities *(cont.)*

ENJOYING THE BOOK *(cont.)*

---

10. **Memories.** Divide the class into cooperative learning groups. Ask students to work together to create a "photo album" of the story by drawing pictures of the events in the order that they occurred. You may wish to have some groups make their album from Rose's point of view, while others make their album from Blanche's point of view. Then lead a discussion during which students examine how the different points of view affected the albums.

EXTENDING THE BOOK

---

1. **Folk Tale Comparison Chart.** Divide the class into cooperative learning groups. Have students fill in the chart for *The Talking Eggs* and another folk tale of their choice (page 10). Have the groups discuss how the folk tales are similar and how they are different.

2. **Math Games.** Have students play Mankala (page 51), a game played by counting beans, and Nsikwi (page 53), a game played to practice multiplication.

3. **Paideia Seminar.** Conduct a Paideia seminar (pages 48–49) to give students an opportunity to express their thoughts and opinions about the story.

4. **Comic Strips.** Another way to improve your students' ability to sequence events is to have them rewrite the main events of the story as a comic strip. After students have created their comic strip using pictures and words, ask them to cut it apart so each event is on a separate cell. Have students place their comic strip in an envelope and trade with a partner. Have the partners put each other's comic strip together in the correct order.

5. **Folk Tale.** Ask students to write and illustrate their own folk tale about some talking eggs, using a story filmstrip (page 68).

6. **Theater Arts.** Have students prepare and present a skit or puppet show about one of the stories (page 69–70). They may wish to use simple costumes, props, and scenery when presenting a skit. They may wish to set up a stage that they can hide behind when presenting a puppet show.

7. **Egg Art.** Three different types of art projects are suggested that can be used with the whole class or by individuals at a learning center (page 14).

8. **Opposing Viewpoints.** Have students work together to write a class book of opposing viewpoints. On one side of the book, have them write the story from Blanche's point of view. On the other side, have them write the story from Rose's point of view.

9. **Interview.** Divide the class into groups. Have one student be a news reporter. Have the other students be characters in the book. Have students write and role-play an interview.

10. **Recipes.** Have students experience cultural diversity by preparing an African recipe for the class to taste (page 71).

11. **Story Filmstrip.** Have students recycle by making their own filmstrip of the story (page 68).

12. **Culminating Activity.** Students make a mural that shows major story events (page 74).

Sequencing

Some of the events from the story are listed below. Use the egg shapes below to rewrite them in the order as they happened.

- Valuable things, such as diamonds and gold coins, spilled out of the plain eggs.
- Blanche ran away from home and went to the old woman's cabin.
- Rose took the jeweled and fancy eggs.
- Blanche saw many strange things, such as a two-headed cow.
- The widow made Blanche do all the work.
- A long time ago there was a widow with two daughters.
- Blanche scooped up the plain eggs to take home.
- Rose took the old woman's head.
- Blanche went to the city to live like a grand lady.
- Rose laughed at all the strange things she saw.
- Horrible creatures came out of the fancy eggs.
- Rose went to find the old woman's cabin.

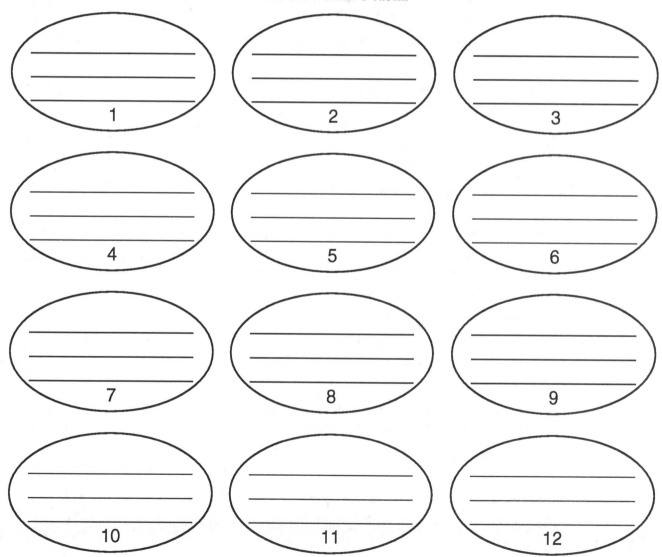

Polar Opposites

After reading *The Talking Eggs*, try this polar opposites rating activity to evaluate the characters and events in the story. Then write information from the story that provides evidence to support the rating you have chosen.

Here is an example: An egg is a _____ object.
                          1   ②   3   4   5
                       fragile   *sturdy*

Evidence: When Blanche and Rose picked up the eggs, they did not break. However, when they dropped the eggs over their shoulders, the shells broke open.

---

1. Rose was a _____ person.
   1   2   3   4   5
   generous   *greedy*

   Evidence:

2. Blanche was a _____ girl.
   1   2   3   4   5
   lazy   *hard-working*

   Evidence:

3. The widow was _____ to Blanche.
   1   2   3   4   5
   cruel   *loving*

   Evidence:

4. The old woman was _____ .
   1   2   3   4   5
   foolish   *wise*

   Evidence:

5. The old woman's animals were _____ .
   1   2   3   4   5
   unusual   *ordinary*

   Evidence:

6. The old woman's plain eggs were _____ .
   1   2   3   4   5
   worthless   *valuable*

   Evidence:

7. When Rose went to the old lady's cabin, she was _____ .
   1   2   3   4   5
   rude   *polite*

   Evidence:

8. Rose was _____ by what came out of the eggs.
   1   2   3   4   5
   bored   *surprised*

   Evidence:

Folk Tale Comparison Chart

Use the chart shown below to compare three folk tales. The first column is done for you. Work with two or three other students to complete the second column using *The Talking Eggs*. Then select a third folk tale and complete the last column of the chart. Discuss how these folk tales are similar and how they are different.

Title and Author	*Cinderella* by Charles Perrault (translated by Marcia Brown)	*The Talking Eggs*	
Culture of Origin	French		
Setting (Time/Place)	Cinderella's house, the prince's palace		
Characters and Character Traits	Cinderella — hard-working, sweet, kind Fairy godmother — kind, generous, understanding Father — spineless Stepmother — cruel, jealous, proud Stepsisters — cruel, self-centered, selfish Prince — charming, loving, determined		
Problem	Cinderella wants to go to the ball, but she has nothing to wear. Her stepmother and stepsisters hate her and insist that she stay home to clean the house while they go to the ball.		
Solution	The fairy godmother gives Cinderella the things she needs to go to the ball. She and the prince fall in love and marry. She forgives her stepsisters and invites them to live in the palace.		
Story Purpose	To teach the lesson that good will win over evil		

10

"Eggsamining" Weights

Write a hypothesis about the relationship between an egg's size and weight. _____

_____

Try the following activity to test your hypothesis. Carefully weigh each of three small eggs, three medium eggs, and three large or jumbo eggs, using a metric scale. Then determine the average weight for each type of egg. Record your data in the following chart.

Egg Weights

	Small Eggs	Medium Eggs	Large or Jumbo Eggs
Egg 1			
Egg 2			
Egg 3			
Average Weight			

Now use your data to create a bar graph that shows the average weight for each type of egg.

Average Weight in Grams

Types of Eggs

What can you conclude about the hypothesis you wrote at the beginning of this activity? _____

_____

Story Pyramid

Use a story pyramid to describe important information from a story, such as the main character, the setting, and the major events in the plot. Carefully choose your words in order to provide a precise description. You may wish to use a dictionary and a thesaurus.

Here are the directions for writing a story pyramid:

Capitalize the first word in each line.

Line 1 — *one word, stating the name of main character*
Line 2 — *two words, describing the main character*
Line 3 — *three words, describing the setting*
Line 4 — *four words, stating the problem*
Line 5 — *five words, describing one event*
Line 6 — *six words, describing a second event*
Line 7 — *seven words, describing third event*
Line 8 — *eight words, stating the solution to the problem*

Here is an example of a story pyramid:

Cinderella
Poor, beautiful
Town with castle
Forbidden to attend ball
Fairy godmother helps her go
Cinderella loses her slipper at midnight
Unique glass slipper fits only Cinderella's foot
Cinderella marries Prince and lives happily ever after

Create your own story pyramid using the example above as a guide. On a separate piece of paper, make a large pyramid shape. In the shape, write a story pyramid for *The Talking Eggs*. If you wish, fill the area around the outside of the pyramid with an illustration representing the subject of the story pyramid.

Cause and Effect

Events are the result of a cause-and-effect relationship. The cause is the reason the event occurred. The effect is what happened as a consequence of the cause. Work with two or three other students to determine the missing causes or effects in the chart below.

Cause	Effect
1. The mother liked Rose best.	1.
2.	2. Blanche got the old woman a drink.
3. The water Blanche brought home from the well was warm.	3.
4.	4. The old woman came down the path and invited Blanche to come home with her.
5. Blanche saw some strange creatures, such as a cow with two heads.	5.
6.	6. Blanche and the old woman had soup for dinner.
7. The old woman told Blanche to take only the eggs that said, "Take me."	7.
8.	8. Valuables, such as diamonds and gold coins, spilled out of the eggs.
9. Rose and the mother were jealous of Blanche.	9.
10.	10. Creatures from the fancy eggs chased Rose and the mother.

Egg Art

You may wish to use the following art activities with your entire class or set up one activity at a time in a learning center.

Talking Eggs

Materials: hard-boiled eggs, markers, poster paint, glue, glitter, fake jewels, beads, sequins, ribbon, a shallow box with hay or cellophane grass in it

Directions: Place the box on a desk or table and put some of the plain hard-boiled eggs into it. Have students use a variety of materials to decorate other hard-boiled eggs to look like the fancy eggs described in the story. When the fancy eggs are dry, place them into the box with the plain eggs. Ask students to work with a partner to write a conversation between a plain egg and a fancy egg. Display the conversations on the wall above the box of eggs.

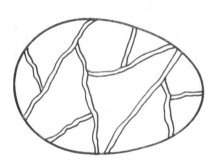

Puzzled Eggs

Materials: white construction paper, scissors, pencil, white glue, a variety of colored chalk

Directions: Cut a piece of white construction paper into a large egg shape. Use a pencil to draw a variety of lines that divide the inside of the egg into small sections. Squeeze white glue over the lines and along the edge of the egg shape. Allow the glue to dry overnight. When the glue is dry, it will be clear but still visible. Fill in each section of the egg shape with colored chalk.

Egg Candles

Materials: bowl, raw egg, pan, paraffin, pieces of crayon, twine or string, small cup, paintbrushes, oil paints

Directions: Carefully poke a small hole at one end of the raw egg while holding it over a bowl. At the other end of the egg, make a larger hole. Pour out the contents of the egg through the larger hole into the bowl. Gently rinse the eggshell with water. Allow the shell to dry. Thread the twine or string through the small hole in the shell to make a wick. Place the eggshell, with the large hole at the top, into the cup. Under the supervision of an adult, melt the paraffin and color it with the crayon wax. Holding the wick in the center, pour the hot wax into the eggshell. As the wax in the shell cools and shrinks, add more hot wax until the eggshell is full. After the candle has completely cooled, carefully crack and peel away the shell. Trim the wick, and decorate the candle using oil paints.

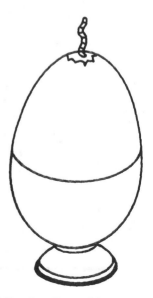

14

Roll of Thunder, Hear My Cry

by Mildred Taylor

Summary

This is the compelling story of an African-American family named the Logans. They are trying to survive in Mississippi during the Great Depression. The story describes one year of Cassie Logan's life. In that year, Cassie experiences the pain of discrimination and public humiliation. Through it all, Cassie shows great courage and remains proud of who she is.

The outline below is a suggested plan for using the various activities presented in this section of *African Americans*. Each lesson can take from one to several days to complete. You should adapt these ideas to fit your own classroom situation.

Sample Plan

Lesson 1
- Prepare a bulletin board (page 75).
- Set the stage (page 16).
- Play Nsikwi (page 53).
- Do a vocabulary activity for chapters 1–3 (page 18).

Lesson 2
- Read chapters 1–3.
- Fill in the story map for chapters 1–3 (page 20).
- Complete a daily writing activity (page 42).
- Compare maps of Africa (page 60).
- Write a poem (pages 43–44).
- Play Mankala (page 51).
- Do a vocabulary activity for chapters 4–6 (page 18).

Lesson 3
- Read chapters 4–6.
- Fill in the story map for chapters 4–6 (page 20).
- Complete a daily writing activity (page 42).
- Make an African recipe (page 71).
- Do a vocabulary activity for chapters 7–9 (page 18).

Lesson 4
- Read chapters 7–9.
- Fill in the story map for chapters 7–9 (page 20).
- Complete a daily writing activity (page 42).
- Write a poem (pages 43–44).
- Do a vocabulary activity for chapters 10–12 (page 18).

Lesson 5
- Read chapters 10–12.
- Fill in the story map for chapters 10–12 (page 20).

- Complete a daily writing activity (page 42).
- Learn to classify (page 25).
- Create a story map (page 20).
- Make a word search (page 45).
- Complete a super box dance (page 46).

Lesson 6
- Complete a daily writing activity (page 42).
- Determine character traits using polar opposites (page 21).
- Create a character map (page 22).
- Write a poem (pages 43–44).
- Predict consequences using a future wheel (page 47).
- Make a Venn diagram (page 59).
- Conduct a Paideia seminar on *Roll of Thunder, Hear My Cry* (pages 48 and 50).

Lesson 7
- Complete a daily writing activity (page 42).
- Examine similes (page 23).
- "Take a Walk in Cassie's Shoes" (page 26).
- Prepare a puppet show (page 69.).
- Produce a story filmstrip (page 68).
- Select culminating activities (pages 72–74).

Lesson 8
- Complete a daily writing activity (page 42).
- Determine the difference between balance and bias (page 24).
- Compare experiences that evoke certain feelings (page 27).
- Present a skit (page 70).
- Complete culminating activities (pages 72–74).

Overview of Activities

SETTING THE STAGE

1. **Bulletin Board.** Prepare the "Working Together" bulletin board suggested on page 75.

2. **Historical Fiction.** Discuss what historical fiction is. Point out that the events described in the story were common in Mississippi during the 1930's. However, the Logans were not a real family, and the situations they faced were probably the combined experiences of several families. Explain that the Logan family was created by the author to help people understand what it felt like to be an African American growing up in the South during the 1930's.

3. **Map.** Have students find Mississippi on a large map of the United States. Discuss how segregation separated African Americans from the rest of the population during the 1930's.

4. **Inquiry Chart.** Have students complete an inquiry chart regarding the Civil Rights Movement. This chart is a helpful way to assess prior knowledge, higher-level thinking skills, and knowledge acquisition. Display the chart on a wall, using a large sheet of butcher paper. The information you record on the chart should include what students know, what they would like to learn, and what they have learned while studying this unit.

5. **Discrimination.** Ask students to choose a number between 0–100 and write it on a piece of paper with their name on it. Collect the papers and explain that the class will be participating in an experiment in discrimination today. Explain that some students will be discriminated against and some will not. Tell students who wrote an odd number to move their desks closer to the back of the room. For part of the day, limit their privileges, place them at the end of the line, and ignore them as much as possible. Tell students who wrote an even number to move their desks closer to the front of the room. Give them normal privileges and pay a great deal of attention to them. At the end of the activity, take time to discuss students' feelings and reactions.

6. **Timeline.** Have students do research to learn historical background information. Have them make a timeline that describes the major events that affected the lives of African Americans (page 39). Ask students to begin the timeline with events from America's colonial period in the 1600's and conclude with events from the 1930's, which is the time period of the story.

ENJOYING THE BOOK

1. **Vocabulary.** Introduce vocabulary for each section of the book. A variety of activities have been suggested to help students learn and retain the vocabulary (page 18).

2. **Word Search.** Have students make a list of twenty words that pertain to the story. Ask them to create a word search (page 45), using those words. Have students trade papers with a partner and solve each other's word search.

3. **Story Map.** Using a story map is an easy way for students to keep track of the most important events in a story (page 20). It considers the basic elements of a story: *setting, problem, sequence* of events, a *solution* to the problem, and the *values* expressed in the story.

Overview of Activities *(cont.)*

ENJOYING THE BOOK *(cont.)*

4. **Polar Opposites.** Students rate the characters and events in the story using a scale of 1 to 5 (page 21). Then they write information from the story that provides evidence to support the rating they have chosen.

5. **Character Map.** Using a graphic organizer (page 22), have students write attributes that describe a character and then give examples from the story as supporting evidence for each attribute. Have students discuss the information they included on their character map.

6. **Similes.** Define what a simile is for students (page 23). Have them locate similes in the story and write what they are used to describe. Then ask students to write sentences in which they use similes to describe something or someone from the story.

7. **Writing Activities.** Assign students a daily writing activity (page 42) or a type of poem (pages 43–44) through which they can express information about the story.

8. **Math Games.** Have students play Mankala (page 51), a game played by counting beans, and Nsikwi (page 53), a game played to practice multiplication.

9. **Reading Comprehension.** Have students identify balances and bias that are in the story (page 24). Then have students explore cause-and-effect relationships from the story and tell what they would do in each situation (page 26).

10. **Classification.** Have students identify five topics to be used as categories. Then have them locate five examples of things from the story that can be classified in each category (page 25).

11. **Paideia Seminar.** Conduct a Paideia seminar (pages 48 and 50) to give students an opportunity to express their thoughts and opinions about the story.

EXTENDING THE BOOK

1. **Responding to Questions.** Present one or more thought-provoking questions to the class. Have students write responses in their journals or discuss the questions (page 19).

2. **Reading.** Have students read poetry by African-American authors, such as Langston Hughes, Phyllis Wheatley, Eloise Greenfield, and Zora Neale Hurston. Have students read other books written by Mildred Taylor.

3. **Theater Arts.** Have students prepare and present a skit or puppet show about one of the stories (pages 69–70). They may wish to use simple costumes, props, and scenery when presenting a skit or a stage that they can hide behind when presenting a puppet show.

4. **Venn Diagram.** Have students use a Venn diagram to compare and contrast characters, places, or events in the story (page 59).

5. **Recipes.** Have students experience cultural diversity by preparing an African recipe for the class to taste (page 71).

6. **Story Filmstrip.** Have students make their own filmstrip of the story (page 68).

7. **Culminating Activity.** Students make a mural of major story events (page 74).

Vocabulary and Activities

Vocabulary

Chapter 1: *meticulously, tormentor, monotonous, admonished, billowed, raucous, briars*

Chapter 2: *formidable-looking, fibrous, ebony, chiffonier, oblivious, bootleg*

Chapter 3: *inaccessible, moronic, relent, conspiratorially, stealthily, occupants, gloat*

Chapter 4: *discourse, mercantile, clapboard, glade, guttural, sharecropping, felling*

Chapter 5: *malevolently, subdued, verandah, retaliate, warily, wheedle, clabber*

Chapter 6: *ominously, languidly, dumbfounded, confounded, aloofness, awestruck, profitable*

Chapter 7: *locusts, aristocracy, caldron, resent, shantytown, eviction, revenue*

Chapter 8: *sentinels, satchel, fallow, flailed, banished, economic, chignon*

Chapter 9: *wisteria, forerunners, furrowed, persnickety, ventured, premature, immobilized*

Chapter 10: *mortgage, ham hocks, lethargically, grating, reproachfully, throng, jauntily*

Chapter 11: *recitation, frenzied, despicable, hastened, lingered, interminable, akimbo*

Chapter 12: *transfixed, desolate, remnants, traipsing, menacingly, flimsy, wan*

Vocabulary Activity Ideas

Provide students with interesting vocabulary activities that will help them learn and retain the vocabulary in *Roll of Thunder, Hear My Cry*. Here are some ideas to try.

1. Have students make a categories chart representing basic parts of speech. Have them list each vocabulary word under the appropriate heading.

2. Divide the class into two teams. Ask both teams to locate a vocabulary word in a section of the book. A team earns a point if they locate the word first. If that team can give the correct definition for the word, they earn another point. Continue playing with other vocabulary words. A team wins when they have the greatest number of points at the end of a period of time that you specify.

3. Ask your students to write a story using the vocabulary words. Point out that students should use the vocabulary words in such a way that they have the same meanings as expressed in the story. Have students read their story to the class. Then display the stories in the hallway for other students to enjoy.

4. Have students make a thesaurus, showing synonyms and antonyms for the vocabulary words.

5. Before students enter the classroom, hide index cards around the room, some with vocabulary words written on them and others with definitions on them. When the class arrives, divide students into two teams to play Vocabulary Hide and Seek. Allow students to search the room for a period of time that you designate. Teams can score a point by matching a word with its definition. The winning team is the one with the most points at the end of the time period.

6. Have students use the vocabulary words as their spelling list each week.

7. Ask students to write a section summary using the vocabulary words. Have students trade summaries with a partner and underline or highlight the vocabulary words.

18

Journal and Discussion Questions

A variety of questions that require higher-level thinking skills can be used to stimulate journal writing and class discussions. You can provide students with a list of question to use as they read the book. However, you can also give them one question at a time by presenting it orally or by writing it on the chalkboard or an overhead transparency. Some suggested questions are provided at the bottom of the page. You may wish to use these, have students create their own questions, or generate some of your own.

Using Journals

Having students write their responses to the questions in a journal or reading log is an effective way to improve their writing skills as they gain a better understanding of the story and the historical events described. Explain to students that they can use a journal to record their thoughts, feelings, ideas, and observations. Notes on cultural or historical background information can also be included in the journal. Point out that ideas and notes in a journal can later be used to create plays, debates, stories, songs, and art displays.

Using Discussions

The questions can be used as a catalyst for class or small group discussions, as well as the topic for a debate. Remind the class before a discussion takes place that every student's input is valuable and that everyone has the right to share his or her ideas without being made fun of or criticized.

Suggested Questions

- When can power be powerless?
- When can too much pride be dangerous?
- If racism had a smell, what would it smell like?
- Pick your favorite character from the story. How are you like that character? How are you different from that character?
- How would this story be different if there had been no discrimination during the 1930's?
- Which do you think Cassie would rather have been, fire or water? Why?
- If Cassie were a Native American living in Mississippi during the 1930's, how would her life have been different?
- How would our country be different if Americans of European descent had been the slaves and Americans of African descent had been the slave owners?
- How could Cassie teach Lillian Jean a lesson without using violence?
- How were African Americans supposed to behave around Caucasians in the 1930's?
- If slavery had never been an issue in the United States, how would things have been different?
- What would you rename this story?
- How did you feel at the end of the story?
- Why do you think some people are prejudiced?
- What are some things that you can do to fight discrimination?
- What would be the benefits or drawbacks of having students from only one culture attend each school?
- What details make *Roll of Thunder, Hear My Cry* an interesting story?
- How is cooperation among cultures beneficial to society?

Story Map

A story map is an easy way to keep track of the most important events in *Roll of Thunder, Hear My Cry*. As you read, identify the setting and main problem in the story. Then, at the end of each chapter, write one or two sentences to summarize the most important events. After completing the book, fill in the solution at the bottom of the story map. On the back of this page, list story values, such as love, respect, responsibility, and honor. Cite examples from the book as evidence of each story value.

The Setting:

Statement of the Problem:

Major Events by Chapter

#1

#2

#3

#4

#5

#6

#7

#8

#9

#10

#11

#12

Statement of Solution:

Polar Opposites

After reading *Roll of Thunder, Hear My Cry,* try this polar opposites rating activity to evaluate the characters and events in the story. Then write information from the story that provides evidence to support the rating you have chosen.

Here is an example: Cassie is very _____ of who she is.

                               ①   2   3   4   5
                              proud   *ashamed*

Evidence: Cassie refused to get off the sidewalk and walk in the street after she accidentally bumped into Lillian Jean.

1. Cassie is _____ stubborn.

       1   2   3   4   5
     a little   *very*

   Evidence:

2. Little Man was _____ to accept old books.

       1   2   3   4   5
     unwilling   *willing*

   Evidence:

3. Mrs. Logan was a _____ teacher.

       1   2   3   4   5
     terrible   *terrific*

   Evidence:

4. Lillian Jean _____ to be beaten up by Cassie.

       1   2   3   4   5
     deserved   *did not deserve*

   Evidence:

5. The Logan children were _____ to sabotage the Jefferson Davis bus.

              1   2   3   4   5
              wrong   *right*

   Evidence:

6. In the 1930's, racism was _____ .

       1   2   3   4   5
     common   *uncommon*

   Evidence:

7. It was _____ that T.J. was taken to jail for the crime he committed.

       1   2   3   4   5
     unfair   *fair*

   Evidence:

8. The ending to this story is a _____ one.

       1   2   3   4   5
     happy   *sad*

   Evidence:

Character Map

Choose a character from *Roll of Thunder, Hear My Cry* and place his or her name in the center square. In the connecting ovals, write attributes that describe that character. In the rectangles, provide evidence from the story for each attribute you list.

Example:

| T.J. |—(lazy)—| would rather cheat than study for a test |

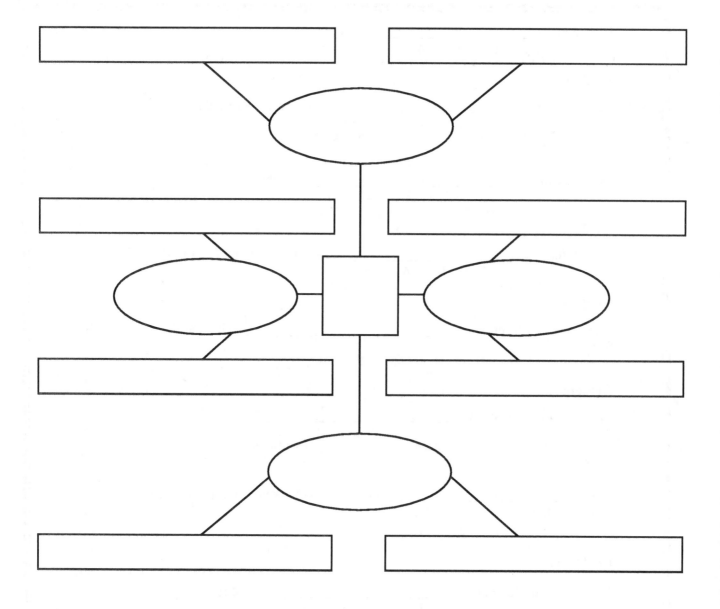

Similes

A simile compares two things using the words *like* or *as*. "Like cat eyes in the night..." is a simile that the author, Mildred Taylor, used to describe the headlights of a car.

Locate the following similes in the book. Then write what each simile is used to describe.

1. "...wound like a lazy serpent...." *(page 6)* —
2. "...work like a woman of twenty...." *(page 7)* —
3. "...spewing clouds of red dust like a huge yellow dragon breathing fire." *(page 13)* —
4. "...slipped like lightning...." *(page 33)* —
5. "..., like a lopsided billy goat on its knees." *(page 54)* —
6. "...chattering like a cockatoo." *(page 104)* —
7. "Grinning like a Cheshire cat...." *(page 179)* —
8. "...like oil on water...." *(page 225)* —

Now write similes to describe each of the following.

1. a field of cotton —
2. Great Faith School —
3. the old textbooks —
4. Papa's pipe —
5. Cassie —
6. Lillian Jean —
7. Little Man —
8. Mr. Morrison —

Balanced or Biased?

Many people experience discrimination in their daily lives. Cassie Logan had to deal with racial bias from the Simms. The Logans also felt discrimination from Harlan Granger and others. Sometimes discrimination is directed towards a person's race (as with Cassie) and sometimes towards a person's gender.

Read the following statements and decide if there is a bias or prejudice. Check the appropriate box.

		Gender Bias	Racial Bias	No Bias
1.	Boys are naturally better in math than girls.	☐	☐	☐
2.	More women than men watch soap operas.	☐	☐	☐
3.	The operation by the lady doctor was a success.	☐	☐	☐
4.	The musicians practiced for the concert.	☐	☐	☐
5.	Asian children make excellent students.	☐	☐	☐
6.	My younger sister reads better than I do.	☐	☐	☐
7.	Moms are better cooks than dads.	☐	☐	☐
8.	Firemen must always be ready to answer the alarm.	☐	☐	☐
9.	Hispanic children are naturally kind.	☐	☐	☐
10.	Tall people have a better view of parades.	☐	☐	☐
11.	Black people have more rhythm than white people.	☐	☐	☐
12.	Women were not allowed to vote until 1920.	☐	☐	☐
13.	Mr. Jones asked the boys to carry the dictionaries to the bookroom while the girls prepared refreshments for the class party.	☐	☐	☐
14.	My dad has an important job, but my mom just stays home.	☐	☐	☐
15.	All nurses should wear clean, appropriate dresses to work.	☐	☐	☐

Hold a class discussion about these statements. Does everyone agree? Write your own definition of bias.

Classification

Classification is the process of arranging things into groups or categories according to common characteristics. In this activity, you will classify information from *Roll of Thunder, Hear My Cry*. First, select a category to write in each oval. Some examples of categories include *prejudice, Great Faith School, foods,* and *jobs*. Then use information from the book to give five examples of things that can be classified in each category. Write these examples, using words or phrases, in the rectangles that are connected to each oval. The first one has been done for you.

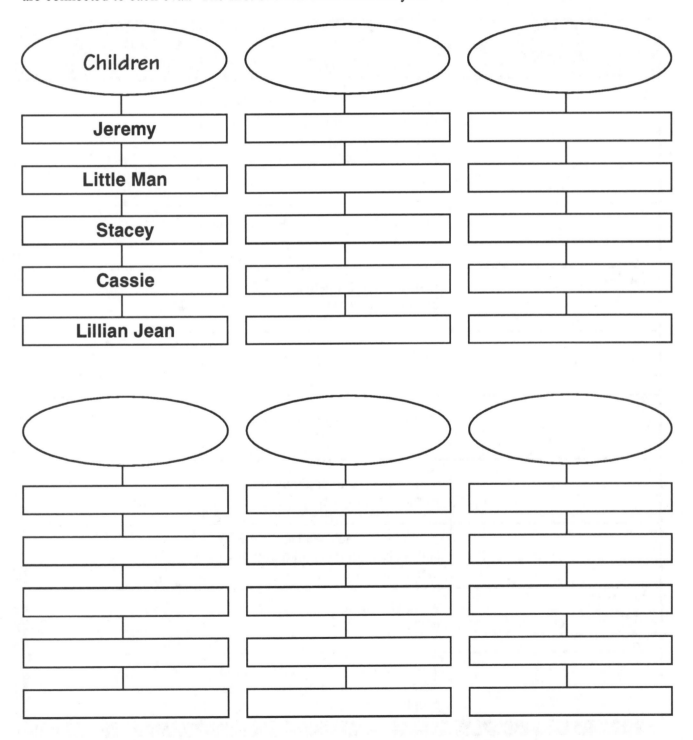

Take a Walk in Cassie's Shoes

Studying cause-and-effect relationships can help you better understand the story. The cause describes why something happened. The effect describes what happened, or the result of the cause. In the middle of the following chart, you will find examples of what Cassie did in response to certain situations. Cassie's reactions are the effects. Write the cause, or reason, for each of Cassie's actions in the first column. Then pretend that you are facing the same set of circumstances. Write the effect, or what you would do, in the third column.

Cause	What Cassie Did (Effect)	What I Would Do
	spoke up for Little Man when he threw the used textbook on the floor	
	refused to accept used textbooks	
	did not tell her parents about the bus incident	
	yelled at Mr. Barnett for discriminating against her	
	apologized again for bumping into Lillian Jean	
	beat up Lillian Jean for revenge	
	told Uncle Hammer about Mr. Barnett pushing her	
	tried to tell Kaleb Wallace that R.W. and Melvin Simms broke into the mercantile with T.J.	
	went with Stacey to help bring T.J. home	
	questioned why African Americans were treated differently from white people	

Cassie and You

Throughout the story you can find examples of how Cassie's actions reflect what she feels. In the column under Cassie's name, write a brief paragraph describing a situation in which Cassie exhibited each of the feelings shown in the chart. Then fill in your name at the top of the last column. Finally, write a few sentences to tell about times when you experienced these feelings.

Feelings	Cassie	_____ (your name)
Fear		
Pride		
Courage		
Hope		
Sadness		
Happiness		
Impatience		
Anger		
Embarrassment		
Love		

One More River to Cross

by Jim Haskins

Summary

This is the story of twelve Americans who had the courage to fight against incredible odds to make their dreams come true. All of them had the determination and commitment to succeed despite the obstacles they had to encounter and the hardships they had to endure.

The outline below is a suggested plan for using the various activities presented in this section of *African Americans*. Each lesson can take from one to several days to complete. You should adapt these ideas to fit your own classroom situation.

Sample Plan

Lesson 1
- Set the stage (page 29).
- Compare two maps of Africa (page 60).
- Read Attucks and Walker stories from *One More River to Cross.*
- Fill in the appropriate sections of the hero comparison chart (page 40).
- Complete a daily writing activity (page 42).
- Do the activity about Walker (page 32).
- Complete the super box dance activity (page 46).
- Write a poem (pages 43–44).

Lesson 2
- Read Henson and Anderson stories.
- Fill in the appropriate sections of the hero comparison chart (page 40).
- Complete a daily writing activity (page 42).
- Label a map of the Arctic (page 33).
- Build an insulator (page 57).
- Make a compass (page 58).
- Describe experiences with discrimination (page 34).
- Identify types of discrimination (page 31).
- Begin research projects (page 76).

Lesson 3
- Read Bunche and Drew stories.
- Fill in the appropriate sections of the hero comparison chart (page 40).
- Complete a daily writing activity (page 42).
- Tell about the meaning of peace (page 35).
- Learn about the parts of blood (page 36).
- Write a poem (pages 43–44).
- Determine possible consequences on a future wheel (page 47).
- Play African–American Concentration (pages 61–65).

Lesson 4
- Read Bearden and Hamer stories.
- Fill in the appropriate sections of the hero comparison chart (page 40).
- Complete a daily writing activity (page 42).
- Create story filmstrips about influential African Americans (page 68).
- Write a poem (pages 43–44).
- Learn about the Kwanzaa celebration (pages 66–67).

Lesson 5
- Read Robinson and Chisholm stories.
- Fill in the appropriate sections of the hero comparison chart (page 40).
- Complete a daily writing activity (page 42).
- Show how a bill becomes a law (page 37).
- Prepare a skit (page 70).
- Complete research projects (page 76).
- Make a word search (page 45).
- Decode the names of famous Americans (page 52).
- Select culminating activities (pages 72–74).

Lesson 6
- Read Malcolm X and Ronald McNair stories.
- Fill in the appropriate sections of the hero comparison chart (page 40).
- Complete a daily writing activity (page 42).
- Create an award (page 38).
- Take a career survey (page 41).
- Make a Venn diagram (page 59).
- Present a puppet show (page 69).
- Complete culminating activities (pages 72–74).

Overview of Activities

SETTING THE STAGE

1. **SSR.** Reserve 15 minutes each day for SSR (sustained, silent reading) of biographies. See the bibliography (pages 77-78) for the titles of some biographies.

2. **Bulletin Board.** This bulletin board provides an activity for students in which they do research to learn about famous African Americans (page 75).

3. **Maps.** Have students obtain background information about Africa by comparing a climate map with a population map (page 60).

4. **Timeline.** Have students do research to learn historical background information. Have them make a timeline that describes the major events that affected the lives of African Americans (page 39). Ask students to begin the timeline with events from America's colonial period in the 1600's and conclude with events from contemporary times. If students started a timeline before reading *Roll of Thunder, Hear My Cry,* have them add events that occurred from the 1930's until the present time. An alternative to this activity is to have students use the timeline to show the contributions of one or more famous African Americans.

5. **Inquiry Chart.** Have students complete an inquiry chart regarding the Civil Rights Movement if they have not already done this before reading *Roll of Thunder, Hear My Cry.* This chart is a helpful way to assess prior knowledge, higher-level thinking skills, and knowledge acquisition. Display the chart on a wall using a large sheet of butcher paper. The information you record on the chart should include what students know, what they would like to learn, and what they have learned while studying this unit.

6. **Newspaper.** Have students use the daily newspaper to create a current events bulletin board that shows the contributions that are being made by Americans from different cultures.

ENJOYING THE BOOK

1. **Hero Comparison Chart.** After students read each story, have them fill in the appropriate part of the Hero Comparison Chart on page 40. After completing the book, facilitate a whole group discussion regarding the traits that these successful people shared.

2. **Story Related Activities.** After students read the stories, have them complete the related activities (pages 32-38). In these activities, students will have the opportunity to write a summary, draw a diagram of an invention they would like to build, label a map of the Arctic, tell about a personal experience when they took a stand against discrimination, describe what peace means to them, identify the different parts of blood, make a flow chart to show how a bill becomes a law, and create an award to celebrate a hero's greatest achievement.

3. **Biographies.** Discuss the difference between a biography and an autobiography. Then have students pick a partner. Ask the partners to interview each other and then write a short biography about the person they interviewed. Have students share their biographies with the class.

4. **Venn Diagram.** Have students use a Venn diagram to compare and contrast the real-life heroes in the stories (page 59).

Overview of Activities *(cont.)*

ENJOYING THE BOOK *(cont.)*

5. **Writing Activities.** Assign students a daily writing activity (page 42) or a type of poem (pages 43–44) through which they can express information about the story.

6. **Concentration.** Have students make a game of African-American Concentration in which they must match pictures with biographical information about famous African Americans (pages 61–65). Challenge students to make similar games using the pictures and biographical information about individuals from other culture groups, such as Asians or Native Americans.

7. **Word Search.** Have students make a list of twenty words that pertain to the stories or a list of twenty names of famous African Americans. Ask them to create a word search (page 45), using those words or names. Have students trade papers and solve each other's word search.

8. **Identifying Discrimination.** Have student describe examples of racial, religious, gender, and age discrimination (page 31).

EXTENDING THE BOOK

1. **Research Center.** Have students identify their own cultural backgrounds and display this information with their pictures in the center. Then have students do research about the contributions of people from different cultures (page 76).

2. **Career Survey.** Have students work in groups to conduct a career survey of the school. Have them record their information on a graph (page 41).

3. **Story Filmstrip.** Have students create a documentary about a famous African American using a recycled filmstrip (page 68).

4. **A Holiday.** After learning about the African-American holiday of Kwanzaa, have students apply the seven principles to their own lives (pages 66–67).

5. **Examining Words.** Have students use a graphic organizer to show word relationships (page 46).

6. **Theater Arts.** Have students prepare and present a skit or puppet show about one of the stories (pages 69–70). They may wish to use simple costumes, props, and scenery when presenting a skit or a stage that they can hide behind when presenting a puppet show. Another activity students can do is to role-play an interview using information from one of the stories.

7. **Future Wheel.** Students predict the possible consequences of their actions using a future wheel (page 47).

8. **Science Experiments.** Have students build an insulator (page 57) and a compass (page 58) after reading about Matthew Henson's expeditions in the Arctic.

9. **Use a Grid.** Have students use coordinates on a grid to decode the names of some famous African Americans (page 52). Challenge students to encode additional names.

10. **Culminating Activities.** Have students participate in a variety of activities at a Cultures Day (page 72), create one or more heritage quilts (page 73), and make a mural about one or more of the stories (page 74).

Understanding Discrimination

Throughout history many people have experienced discrimination. Discrimination occurs as a result of prejudice, or bias. Prejudice is an opinion about a certain group of people based on a single characteristic, such as ethnicity, religion, gender, or age. The kind of prejudice that causes discrimination has at its root an unfavorable opinion which is based on a lack of knowledge and understanding.

The battle against discrimination is still being fought. Use the space below to give examples of discrimination existing today. Newspapers and magazines are excellent sources of information. However, you can also use examples from your personal experiences or interview friends and family members about their experiences.

Examples of Discrimination

Racial:

Religious:

Gender:

Age:

Madam C.J. Walker: A Success Story

After reading about Madam C.J. Walker in *One More River to Cross,* use the space below to write a summary of the story. Then answer the questions.

Summary

- Why do you think Madam C.J. Walker was successful?

_____

- Why do you think Madam C.J. Walker felt education was important?

_____

- If you could be an inventor, what would you create?

_____

On the back of this paper, draw a diagram of an invention that you would like to make.

Matthew Henson Explored the North Pole

Matthew Henson made several expeditions to the Arctic before he actually reached the North Pole in 1909. After reading the story about Matthew Henson in *One More River to Cross*, examine the map shown below. It shows the Arctic expeditions in which Henson participated. Use an atlas or other reference book to label the following places on the map.

North Pole	Robeson Channel	Cape Columbia	Queen Elizabeth Islands
Arctic Ocean	Kennedy Channel	Nares Strait	Greenland
Lincoln Sea	Ellesmere Island	Baffin Bay	Greenland Sea

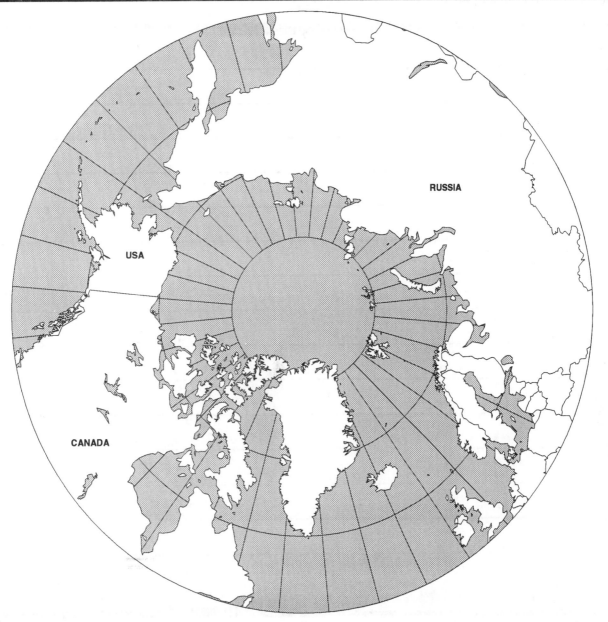

Eleanor Roosevelt Helped Marian Anderson

Mrs. Eleanor Roosevelt, President Franklin D. Roosevelt's wife, was outraged when she learned that Marian Anderson, an African-American opera singer, was denied the opportunity to sing at Constitution Hall based solely on the color of her skin. Mrs. Roosevelt arranged for Ms. Anderson to sing at the Lincoln Memorial. Ms. Anderson's experience is an example of racial discrimination. Mrs. Roosevelt knew that racial discrimination was wrong and that she had to do something about it.

Many people have experienced discrimination during their lives. Different aspects, such as race, religion, gender, age, or disability can cause a person to be the victim of discrimination. When have you or someone you know had to take a stand against discrimination? Explain what happened. If you have never faced discrimination and do not know someone who has, think of what it might be like and write what you would do about it.

Ralph Bunche and the Meaning of Peace

Ralph Bunche actively worked to negotiate peace between Israel and the surrounding Arab countries. He knew that this would be a difficult job since there had been racial and religious bigotry in the Middle East throughout history. As a result of his peace negotiations, Mr. Bunche won the Nobel Peace Prize in 1950. He became the first African American to receive this honor.

After reading the story about Ralph Bunche, think about what peace means to you. Use the space below to describe your definition of peace. Then explain what you can do to make the world a place that is "at peace."

Charles Drew and the Study of Blood

Charles Drew did extensive research with blood. He discovered ways to isolate the parts of blood and store blood plasma that was needed for transfusions. In this activity, you will use reference tools for researching information about the four parts of blood. Take notes in the appropriate spaces below.

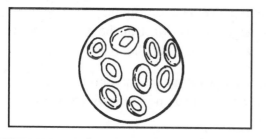

Red Blood Cells

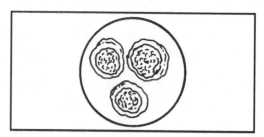

White Blood Cells

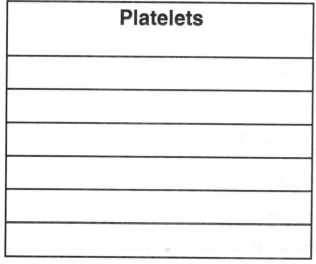

Platelets

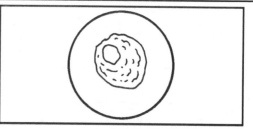

Plasma

Shirley Chisholm as a Member of Congress

As a member of the United States Congress, Shirley Chisholm worked to make bills become laws. Use an encyclopedia or other reference book to locate information about how a bill becomes a law. Then use the flow chart below to describe what happens in each step of this process.

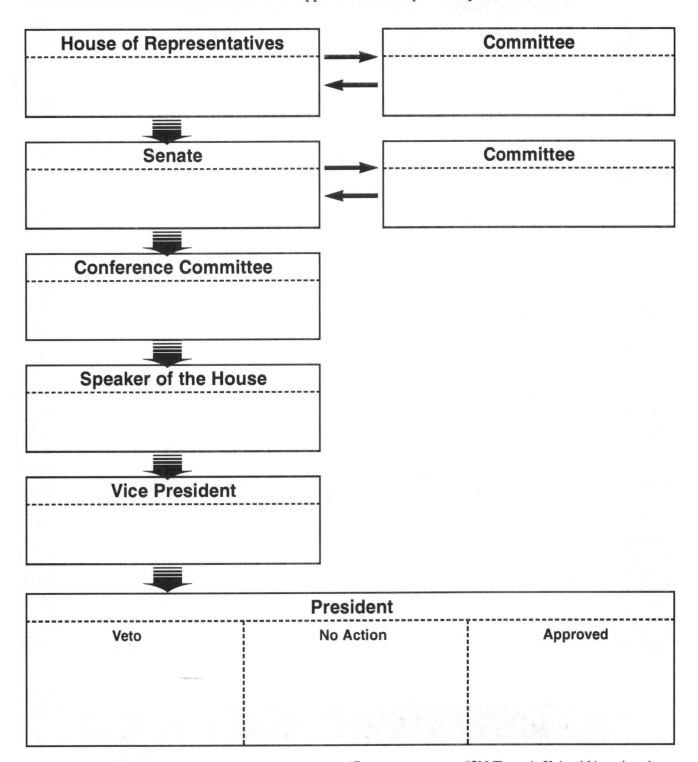

An Award for Ronald McNair

Dr. Ronald McNair had many impressive accomplishments during his short lifetime. What do you think was his most important achievement? Use pictures and words to make an award that honors McNair for his contributions to the space program.

Timeline

In this activity, you will work with three or four other students to make a timeline. You can use this timeline in any of the following ways: to show historical events that affected African Americans, to show the contributions of famous African Americans, or to show the important events in one African American's life. Prepare your timeline by carefully cutting out the timeline strips and taping them end to end.

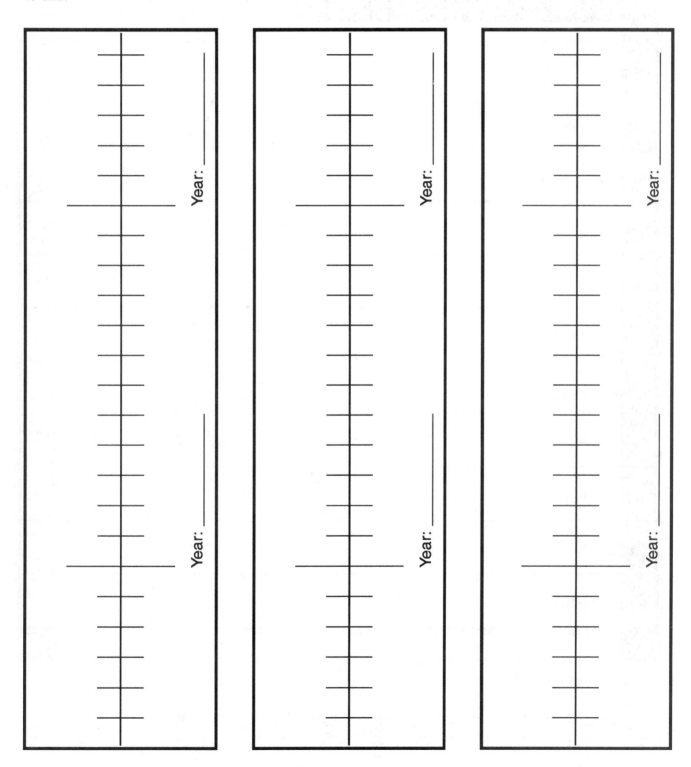

Hero Comparison Chart

Fill in the following hero comparison chart after reading each story in *One More River To Cross*.

Hero's Name	Family	Education	Interests	Obstacles	Achievements
Crispus Attucks					
Madam C.J. Walker					
Matthew Henson					
Marian Anderson					
Ralph Bunche					
Charles R. Drew					
Romare Bearden					
Fannie Lou Hamer					
Eddie Robinson					
Shirley Chisholm					
Malcolm X					
Ronald McNair					

When your chart is complete, look for similarities and differences among the heroes. What traits do you think most heroes have in common?

_____

_____

Career Survey

In this activity you will determine who is interested in the careers described in *One More River to Cross*. Work in groups of three or four to conduct a career survey of the students at your school. Make a chart that shows the classes that each group will survey. This will help you avoid surveying the same class twice. If you have an especially large school, you may wish to limit your survey to certain grade levels.

When surveying students, make a tally mark next to the career that they think they might be interested in pursuing. If students are not interested in any of these careers, place a tally mark next to "None of the Above" located at the bottom of the chart. After completing the survey, count the tally marks to get a total for each career. Then follow the directions shown below the chart.

Artist	
Astronaut	
Civil Rights Activist	
Diplomat	
Explorer	
Football Coach	
Inventor	
Legislator	
Entertainer	
Patriot/Soldier	
Political Leader	
Scientist	
None of the Above	

Use the data that you collected from the survey to make a pictograph or a bar graph. If you present your data in a pictograph, be sure to include a key that tells the value of each symbol. If you present your data in a bar graph, be sure to mark and number the bottom line to show increments that can be used to tell how many students were interested in each career. Use the samples below as a guide.

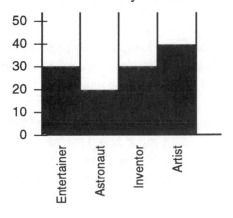

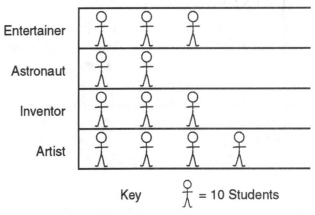

Daily Writing Activities

Select a writing activity from the following suggestions or create one of your own.

✏️ Sequels

Write a sequel to *Roll of Thunder, Hear My Cry* or *The Talking Eggs,* or write another story that could be added to *One More River to Cross.*

✏️ Letters

Write a letter to one of the people or characters in the stories you have read. You may wish to ask that person about events that happened in the story.

✏️ Diary

Pretend you are one of the characters that you have read about in this unit. Write a diary entry telling what you think and feel about your situation as that character.

✏️ Dialogue

Write a dialogue between the fictional characters or real-life heroes described in the reading selections for this unit.

✏️ Comparison

Read other books by the same author. Write an essay that compares two or more of the author's books.

✏️ Radio

Work with three or four other students to write and present a radio play of one or more parts of a reading selection from this unit. You may wish to include sound effects in your radio play. Practice your radio play using a tape recorder.

✏️ Historical Fiction

Select a period of history or an event from history. Do research and take notes about that time period or event. Then write a story that is historical fiction. Be sure to include some of the facts you learned while researching.

✏️ A Song

Work with two or three other students to write a song. The song can be a tribute to a specific African American, or it an be about a topic presented in this unit, such as equality, justice, and pride.

✏️ Newspaper Article

Look at some front-page articles in a newspaper. Front-page articles are about important people and current events. Notice how these articles answer questions, such as *who, what, when, where, how,* and *why.* Pretend that you are a newspaper reporter. You have been asked to write a front-page article about the contributions of an African American. Select the person that you want to write about. You can use one of the African Americans named as a research topic on page 76, or described in *One More River to Cross,* or you can pick one of your own. Do some research to learn more about the person you have chosen. Then write a front-page article about that person. No matter which person your article is about, write about him or her as if you have just witnessed that person's contribution being made.

Poetry

Writing poetry can be fun and a creative way to express ideas. Some or all of the types of poetry can be used with each of the reading selections in this unit. You can present these poetry lessons to the whole class using an overhead projector or chalkboard.

When presenting poetry lessons for the first time, follow these steps:

Step 1: Introduce the type of poetry to be studied.

Step 2: Present an example of this type of poetry. You may wish to use one of the examples that have been provided here and on page 44, or you can use one of your own.

Step 3: Provide students with guided practice by creating one or more poems with the entire class.

Step 4: Have students work independently, with a partner, or in a cooperative learning group to write a poem.

After students become familiar with the different types of poetry, you can use these examples on a bulletin board or in a learning center.

Clerihew

A clerihew is a humorous poem about a person. It was invented by Edward Clerihew Bentley, an English mystery writer. The first line of a clerihew ends with the person's name. The second line rhymes with the first and tells something about the person. The third and fourth lines rhyme with each other and tell something about the person, too.

> *There goes a boy named Stacey Logan,*
> *He thinks he'll have some fun.*
> *He brings the school bus to a screeching halt,*
> *Without anyone knowing who's at fault.*

Diamonte

This verse has seven lines and is diamond-shaped. It begins with one topic and ends with a completely different topic. To write a diamonte, begin each word with a capital letter and follow these directions.

Line 1 is a noun. It is the subject of the poem.

Line 2 has two words that describe the subject.

Line 3 contains three "-ing" words that describe the subject.

Line 4 has two short phrases. The first phrase describes the original subject and the second phrase describes a new subject that is often the opposite of the original subject.

Line 5 uses three "-ing" words about the new subject.

Line 6 contains two words that describe this new subject.

Line 7 names the new or opposite subject.

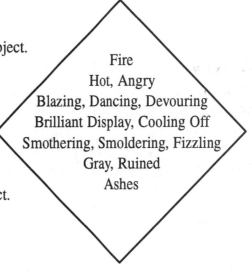

Fire
Hot, Angry
Blazing, Dancing, Devouring
Brilliant Display, Cooling Off
Smothering, Smoldering, Fizzling
Gray, Ruined
Ashes

Poetry *(cont.)*

Couplet

The *couplet* is a two-line verse. The last word in each line rhymes. A poem can be made up of one or more couplets.

> *The rabbits danced away the night,*
> *Then disappeared at morning's light.*

Limerick

A *limerick* is a comical poem consisting of five lines. Lines 1, 2 and 5 rhyme and lines 3 and 4 rhyme.

> *There once was a young girl named Rose,*
> *Who dreamed of great wealth and fine clothes.*
> *So exceedingly vain,*
> *Was this very "plain Jane,"*
> *That to others she would snub her nose!*

List Poem

In a *list poem* the first line is the title and consists of a word or phrase stating the main idea. Then there are several short statements that tell the author's feelings about the main idea.

> *What makes me happy*
> *Reaching my goals,*
> *Making others smile,*
> *Being accepted for*
> *who and what I am,*
> *Ice cream sundaes*
> *on a hot summer day,*
> *Having others call me friend.*

Acrostic

The *acrostic* has been around for centuries. To write an acrostic, write a word, phrase, or name down the left side of the paper. Then write a series of word or phrases that describe the topic or give your feelings about it. Each line begins with a letter of the name or subject.

> *Beauty sometimes*
> *Lies below the surface. Look*
> *At the inside*
> *Not the*
> *Covering. You might find*
> *Hidden an*
> *Enchanting surprise.*

Alliteration Poem

An alliteration poem uses sound to create a special effect. To create an alliteration poem, choose words that begin with the same sound. Try writing three lines of poetry with alliteration in each line. The trick is to make all the words start with the same sound.

> *Terrible, taunting Tom*
> *Took the test*
> *Two times two.*

Language Arts

Word Search

In this activity, you will create a word search. First use the box at the top to make a list of the twenty words that will be in your word search. Then write the letters of those words in the boxes below, one letter in each box. Words can be written horizontally, vertically, or diagonally in the boxes. After you have made your word search, trade with a partner and locate each other's words.

For this word search, you may use twenty words from one of the following:

- *The Talking Eggs*
- *Roll of Thunder, Hear My Cry*
- *One More River to Cross*
- the names of famous African Americans

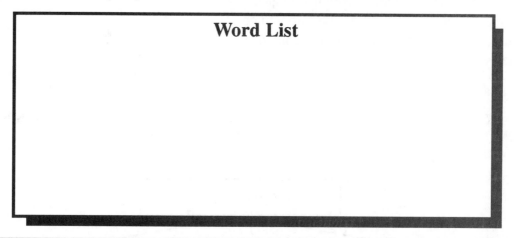

Word List

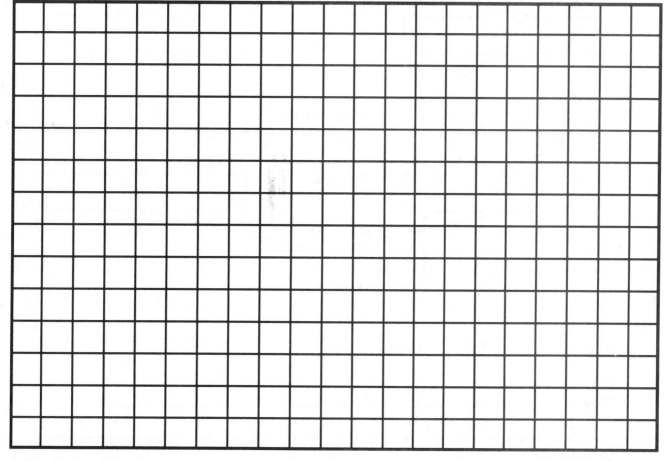

Super Box Dance

In this activity, you will use a graphic organizer to show word relationships. In the box at the top, write a word that describes one of the topics discussed in this unit. Examples include *racism, freedom,* and *discrimination.* Think about that word and what it means. Write two words in the second layer of boxes that you think relate to the topic you picked for the top box. Now think only about the word that you wrote in the box on the left. Write two words that are related in the connecting boxes that are in the third layer. Do the same for the word that you wrote in the second layer box on the right. Continue the process in the fourth layer by writing a word that relates to each set of two words that is in the third layer. Fill in the final box with a word that relates to the two words in the fourth layer. Be sure you do not use any word more than once. Write a sentence that relates your first word to your last word.

Now fill in a super box dance on your own. Use the example on the right as a guide.

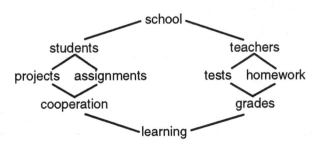

Sentence: School is where students go to learn.

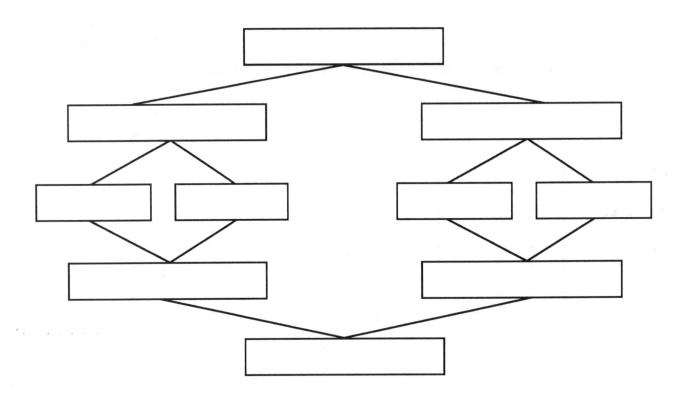

Sentence: _____

_____

Future Wheel

Use this graphic organizer to study the process of decision making. Follow the steps below.

- **Step 1:** Write a topic in the center rectangle.
- **Step 2:** In the extending ovals, write the immediate effects caused by the original action. You may wish to draw additional extending ovals if they are needed.
- **Step 3:** In the extending triangles, write the immediate effects caused by the effects written in the ovals. You may wish to draw additional extending triangles if they are needed.
- **Step 4:** Use the information in the future wheel to write a short paragraph that will persuade a friend to make the best choice.

Example

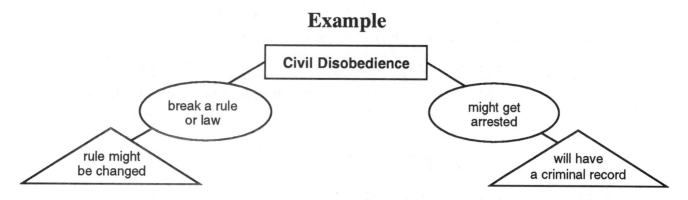

Now make a few of your own future wheels. Here are some suggested topics: prejudice against minorities, slavery, racism, affirmative action, civil disobedience, and reverse discrimination.

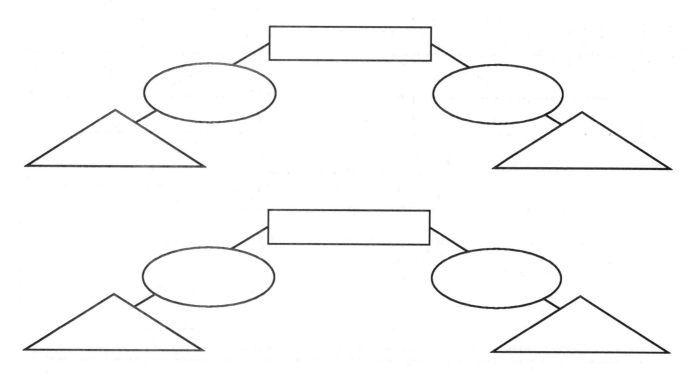

Paideia

Teacher Background

The original idea for Paideia is over 2,000 years old. The concept was first described by Socrates. In the early 1980's Mortimer Adler developed the idea and was the first to establish Paideia in Chicago's schools. Currently, there are over 125 schools nationwide using the Paideia method.

Paideia means "the upbringing of a child." This method helps children in kindergarten through twelfth grade learn to think independently about areas of study, such as literature, art, and mathematics. They learn to express ideas about the meaning of their studies and to enhance these ideas by considering other people's opinions and interpretations. An essential part of the program is a method of discussion called a seminar. In the seminar, teachers guide students as they work together to answer questions about the themes and meanings of the reading selections. Throughout this process, students develop their own opinions about what they have read, and they must support their opinions with evidence from the text.

Steps for conducting a seminar:

❖ **Step 1:** Chairs or desks should be placed in a circle or semicircle to facilitate discussion.

❖ **Step 2:** Everyone in the seminar must be prepared by reading the selection.

❖ **Step 3:** The teacher/facilitator prepares for the seminar by developing a list of provocative questions that he/she believes will lead to a deeper understanding of the text.

❖ **Step 4:** After the teacher/facilitator presents the initial question, students lead the discussion.

❖ **Step 5:** Teachers/facilitators never give answers; they simply oversee the discussion and direct students to substantiate their opinions.

❖ **Step 6:** There are no right or wrong answers in a seminar. Everyone's opinion is valid but must be supported with evidence from the text.

❖ **Step 7:** Everyone is asked to take an active role in the seminar.

❖ **Step 8:** To encourage freedom of discussion, no one needs to raise a hand in order to speak. However, no one is allowed to interrupt another person who is speaking.

Use page 49 for a Paideia Curriculum Plan for *The Talking Eggs* and page 50 for a Paideia Curriculum Plan for *Roll of Thunder, Hear My Cry*.

More information on the Paideia Curriculum appears in the bibliography on page 77.

Paideia Curriculum Plan I

Seminar Selection: *The Talking Eggs* by Robert D. San Souci

Grade: Intermediate and middle school

Theme: Creole culture, folk tales, kindness and diligence are rewarded—greediness and laziness are punished

Goal: To encourage kindness and good work habits

Core Questions: What happens to people who are kind and hard working? greedy and lazy?

Key Concepts: respect vs. disrespect, hard work vs. laziness, kindness vs. cruelty

Key Skills: reading comprehension, analyzing, drawing conclusions, communicating, substantiating opinions with evidence, synthesizing

Pre-Activities:
> Read the entire book.

Seminar Questions:
1. What lesson did this folk tale teach?
2. Why do you think the lesson was taught using a story format?
3. How would you feel about the story if Rose had been rewarded and Blanche had not?
4. Do you think that this folk tale reflects real life? Explain.
5. Which character would you like to be? Why?

Post Activities:
- Encourage students to read other folk tales. See the bibliography on pages 77 and 78 for suggestions.
- Have students create a mural with the themes and images inspired by this selection.
- Have students write how they felt about the story and then enclose their papers in plastic eggs.
- Have students make a mobile that shows the characters and animals from the story.
- Have students write their own folk tales and use them to teach the class a moral lesson.
- Have students choose classical music that they think fits with this story.

Evaluation Plan:

Students will evaluate their own performances during the seminar.

Teachers will observe student participation in the seminar.

Teachers will observe student participation in the post activities.

Paideia Curriculum Plan II

Seminar Selection: *Roll of Thunder, Hear My Cry* by Mildred Taylor

Grade: Intermediate or middle school

Theme: African Americans, racism, discrimination, conflicts between people, pride, equality

Goal: To encourage fairness, respect, and interracial cooperation

Core Question: What in life is worth fighting for?

Key Concepts: conflicts, cultural diversity

Key Skills: reading comprehension, analyzing, inferring, communicating, substantiating opinions with evidence, synthesizing

Pre-Activities:
> Read the entire book.
> Preview vocabulary.

Seminar Questions:
1. Mr. Morrison says, "Sometimes you just gotta fight." What did he mean by this statement?
2. Are people of different races treated equally?
3. What is the most important lesson to be learned from this book?
4. What feelings are expressed in this book?
5. Did the Logans win or lose the fight against racism?
6. Which character would you like to be? Why?

Post Activities:
- Encourage students to read other books in this series.
- Have students make a big book of the story and share it with a group of younger students.
- Have students draw a series of pictures about the story.
- Have students tell how the story would change if it had been written about contemporary times.
- Have students design an activity folder that gives suggestions for ways to fight discrimination.

Evaluation Plan:

Students will evaluate their own performances during the seminar.

Teachers will observe student participation in the seminar.

Teachers will observe student participation in post activities.

Mankala

Arabs call this game Kalah. They took it to Africa, where it has many different names. In East Africa, it is called Mankala. In West Africa, it is called Owara. In South Africa, it is known as Ohara. No matter which version of the game is used, you and your students will enjoy playing Mankala.

Materials

- clean egg carton
- tape or glue
- bean seeds
- 2 red markers, one for each player

Preparing the Game

You can make this game out of an empty egg carton. Look at the picture on this page. Build the game by separating the top and bottom of the egg carton. Cut the top section in half and attach each half to a side of the bottom section, as shown in the illustration. Each of the two end cups becomes a player's cup, where he or she collects beans (points). The player's cup is on his or her right.

Game Directions

1. Have students pick a partner and sit across from each other. Tell them to put three beans in each of the twelve cups in the egg carton.

2. Have students decide which player goes first. The first player picks out the beans in the cup immediately on his/her left. This player should then put his/her red marker in the empty cup.

3. Going counterclockwise away from the red marker, have the first player place one bean in each cup until all three beans have been used.

4. Look in the cup opposite the cup where the last bean was dropped. Have the first player take those beans out and place them in the end cup to his/her right. These beans are now the first player's points.

5. Tell the second player to do the same thing that the first player just did by repeating the third and fourth steps.

6. When it is the first player's turn again, he/she finds his/her red marker and takes the beans from the cup to the right. That player distributes those beans as described in step 3. If there are no beans in the cup to the right, that player puts his/her red marker into the empty cup, and it becomes the other player's turn. It is important to remember to move the red marker so that you know which cup to start with for your next move.

7. Continue to play until there is only one bean left. The last player to put any beans in his/her end cup gets the last bean.

8. Both players count their beans. The player with the greatest number of beans in his or her cup wins the game.

Using a Grid

Learn interesting facts about some famous African Americans by using a grid to decode the names. Write the letter on the line that corresponds to each set of coordinates. For example, if you are given the coordinates (1,5), you would write the letter "S." (The horizontal coordinate is the first

5	S	A	H	O	P	I
4	I	W	B	L	F	E
3	Q	C	N	E	U	A
2	D	V	J	T	Y	O
1	K	Z	R	G	M	X
	1	2	3	4	5	6

number in the pair and the vertical coordinate is the second number.)

1. __ __ __ __ __ __ __ __ __ __ __ __ __ is famous
   (3,5) (2,5) (3,1) (3,1) (6,5) (6,4) (4,2) (4,2) (5,3) (3,4) (5,1) (6,3) (3,3)
   for freeing more than 300 slaves using the Underground Railroad.

2. __ __ __ __   __ __ __ __ __ refused to give up her bus
   (3,1) (4,5) (1,5) (2,5)   (5,5) (6,3) (3,1) (1,1) (1,5)
   seat to a white person.

3. __ __ __ __ __   __ __ __ __ __ __ __ __
   (3,2) (2,5) (5,1) (4,3) (1,5)   (2,5) (3,1) (5,1) (6,5) (1,5) (4,2) (6,4) (2,5) (1,2)
   was an important spy for the United States during the Revolutionary War.

4. __ __ __ __   __ __ __ __ __ __ __ is a famous
   (5,1) (2,5) (5,2) (2,5)   (6,3) (3,3) (4,1) (6,4) (4,4) (4,5) (5,3)
   performer, writer, and director.

5. __ __ __ __ __   __ __ __ __ __ __ __ owns her
   (4,5) (5,5) (3,1) (2,5) (3,5)   (2,4) (6,5) (3,3) (5,4) (3,1) (4,3) (5,2)
   own television studio.

6. __ __ __ __ __   __ __ __ __ __ __ __ was the first
   (3,2) (4,3) (1,5) (1,5) (4,3)   (3,2) (2,5) (2,3) (1,1) (1,5) (6,2) (3,3)
   African-American man to run for president.

7. __ __ __ __ __ __   __ __ __ __ __ __
   (5,1) (2,5) (3,1) (4,2) (6,5) (3,3)   (4,4) (5,3) (4,2) (3,5) (6,4) (3,1)
   __ __ __ __ , __ __ ., led the fight for civil rights during the 1960's
   (1,1) (1,4) (3,3) (4,1)   (3,2) (3,1)
   and was awarded the Nobel Peace Prize in 1963.

8. __ __ __ __ __ __ __ __ __   __ __ __ __ __
   (1,5) (4,5) (3,2) (4,5) (5,3) (3,1) (3,3) (4,3) (3,1)   (4,2) (3,1) (5,3) (4,2) (3,5)
   was born a slave and escaped. She fought against slavery and for women's voting rights.

9. __ __ __ __ __ __   __   __ __ __ __ __ __ __
   (3,4) (4,5) (4,5) (1,1) (4,3) (3,1)   (4,2)   (2,4) (2,5) (1,5) (3,5) (6,5) (3,3) (4,1)
   __ __ __ started a school to train African-American teachers, farmers,
   (4,2) (6,2) (3,3)
   brick makers, and carpenters.

10. __ __ __ __ __ __   __ __ __ __ __ __ __ __
    (3,2) (2,5) (2,3) (1,1) (6,5) (4,3)   (3,1) (6,2) (3,4) (6,5) (3,3) (1,5) (4,5) (3,3)
    was the first African American to play major league baseball. He joined the Brooklyn Dodgers in 1947.

Nsikwi

Nsikwi is a popular bowling game among Nigerian children. Divide the class into cooperative learning groups. Then use the following directions to have your students play Nsikwi in a way that gives them the opportunity to practice math skills.

You will need the following materials: one orange (or a rubber ball about the size of an orange) for each group, and a dry corn cob for each student.

Directions

- Prepare each corn cob by cutting off the thick end so it is flat and can stand on its end.
- If possible, take students outside. Have each group sit in a large circle.
- Have students stand their corn cobs on end to their left.
- Have students decide who will go first in each group.
- To begin play, have the first student try to knock over another player's corn cob by rolling the orange on the ground. If the student is successful, he or she has the chance to score a point by responding correctly during a specific activity. (See "Ways to Use the Game" for some suggested activities to use with students.) Other students in the group confirm that the response is correct. The student continues to play until he or she misses the question, fails to knock a corn cob down, or has knocked down all of the corn cobs.
- The corn cobs are reset. Play continues as the orange is passed to the left and each student takes his or her turn.
- Have students keep score. The winner is the person with the greatest number of points at the end of a time period that you specify.

Ways to Use the Game

1. Randomly assign each student a number. To score a point and roll again, the student who is taking a turn must multiply his or her number times the number of the person whose corn cob was knocked down.

2. Randomly assign each student a measurement, such as 6 cm, that will represent a rectangle's length or width. To score a point and roll again, the student who is taking a turn must determine the area or the perimeter of a rectangle. (Examples: 6 cm x 8 cm = 48 square cm for the area, or 6 cm + 6 cm + 8 cm + 8 cm = 28 cm for perimeter.)

   Adapt the game to provide students with practice in other math skills areas, such as inequalities or fractions.

3. Prior to the game, have students prepare index cards with math vocabulary on one side and definitions on the other. When it is a student's turn, the stack of cards is placed to his or her right with the word side up. To score a point and roll again, the student who is taking a turn must say the definition of the word on the top card.

"Eggsperiments"

The following fun "Eggsperiments" can be used in conjunction with the reading selection *The Talking Eggs.* You may work by yourself, with a partner, or in a group with other students. Respond to the questions below on the back of this paper.

Is It Magic?

Materials

- a hard-boiled egg
- a jar filled with fresh water
- a jar filled with "ocean" water which is made by mixing 2 tsp. (10 ml) of salt into 2 cups (480 ml) of fresh water

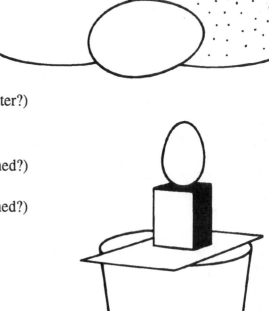

Directions

1. *Write a hypothesis.*
   (What do you think will happen when you put the egg in the fresh water? What do you think will happen when you put the egg in the "ocean" water?)

2. *Test your hypothesis.*

   a. Put the egg into the jar of fresh water. Observe and record your results. (What happened?)

   b. Place the egg into the jar of "ocean" water. Observe and record your results. (What happened?)

3. *Draw conclusions.*
   (How did the salt in the water affect the egg?)

Testing Inertia

Materials

- a glass
- an index card
- sugar
- a hard-boiled egg
- the outer part of a matchbox

Directions

1. *Set up the experiment.* Place some sugar at the bottom of the glass. The sugar will prevent the glass from breaking. Position the card over the top of the glass. Then stand the outer part of the matchbox on its end on top and in the middle of the card. Finally, carefully place the egg on top of the matchbox so that it is balanced.

2. *Write a hypothesis.*
   (What do you think will happen when you flick the card out from between the glass and the matchbox?)

3. *Test your hypothesis.*
   a. Use your thumb and your first finger to flick the card out from between the glass and the matchbox.
   b. Observe and record your results. (What happened?)

4. *Draw conclusions.*
   (Why did the egg end up where it did?)

"Eggsperiments" *(cont.)*

Here are some more fun "Eggsperiments." You may work by yourself, with a partner, or in a group with other students. Respond to the questions below on the back of this paper.

Cooked or Raw?

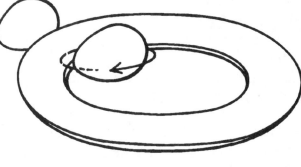

Materials
- a raw egg
- a hard-boiled egg
- a flat surface

Directions

1. *Write a hypothesis.*
   (What will happen if I stop a spinning hard-boiled egg, and then let it go? What will happen if I stop a spinning raw egg, and then let it go?)

2. *Test your hypothesis.*

   a. Carefully spin the hard-boiled egg on a flat surface. While it is still spinning, stop it for a moment, and then let it go.
   Observe and record your results. (What happened?)

   b. Carefully spin the raw egg on a flat surface. While it is still spinning, stop it for a moment, and then let it go.
   Observe and record your results. (What happened?)

3. *Draw conclusions.*
   (Why do you think there was a difference in the results for the cooked egg and for the raw egg?)

Egg in a Bottle

Close adult supervision is essential for this "Eggsperiment."

Materials
- an 8 oz. (250 mL) glass baby bottle without a top
- a small egg (slightly larger than the opening at the top of the bottle) that has been cooked for at least ten minutes
- margarine, butter, or cooking oil
- a paper fan made from a piece of paper that is 4 in. x 4 in. (10 cm x 10 cm)
- matches

Directions
1. Carefully peel the shell off the cooked egg.
2. Rub margarine, butter, or oil all over the egg and around the open top of the bottle.
3. Write a hypothesis. (What do you think will happen when you place the egg on top of the bottle as a paper burns inside the bottle?)
4. HAVE AN ADULT light a match, catch the paper fan on fire, and place it into the bottle.
5. Quickly place the egg on top of the bottle.
6. Observe and record your results. (What happened to the egg?)
7. Draw conclusions. (Why do you think the egg reacted as it did?)

"Eggsperiments" *(cont.)*

Here are some more fascinating "Eggsperiments." You may work by yourself, with a partner, or in a group with other students.

Squeeze an Egg

Materials

- a raw egg that does not have any cracks
- a sink or a plastic washtub

Directions

1. Remove any rings you are wearing from your fingers.
2. Place a raw egg directly in the palm of your hand.
3. Hold your hand over a sink or plastic washtub and squeeze as hard as you can.

You will find that despite its small size, the egg is amazingly strong. The reason it is so hard to break an egg by squeezing is because it is a three-dimensional arch, and the force you use to squeeze with is spread all over the egg.

Egg Engraving

Materials

- a wax crayon
- a hard-boiled egg
- glass or cup
- vinegar
- soft-bristled toothbrush
- scouring powder

Directions

1. Use the crayon to draw a design or write your name on the shell of a hard-boiled egg.
2. Put the egg into a glass.
3. Pour vinegar into the glass until the egg is covered.
4. You will notice bubbles forming on the egg except where the crayon marks are. This is because the crayon protects that part of the shell from the chemical reaction that is taking place.
5. Allow the egg to soak for about two hours or until all the bubbles are gone.
6. Pour out the used vinegar from the glass and pour fresh vinegar in until the egg is covered again.
7. Allow the egg to soak for about four hours.
8. Remove the egg from the glass and use running water to wash it off.
9. Continue running the water, and very carefully use the soft-bristled toothbrush and some scouring powder to rub the crayon wax from the egg.
10. Observe your design or name on the eggshell. It should appear as though it was engraved on the shell.

Build an Insulator

Matthew Henson and the other members of the expedition to the North Pole had to worry about conserving body heat in the extremely cold arctic temperatures. In this activity you will learn how insulation can help store heat.

Materials

- a large jar with the top
- a small jar with the top
- a small glass
- a pitcher with warm water
- cellophane or masking tape
- cork
- two pieces of aluminum foil
- scissors

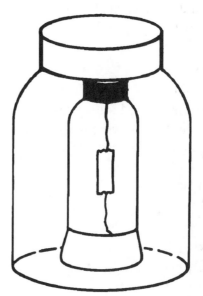

As you do this experiment, remember to:

- Formulate a hypothesis.
- Observe and record your results.
- Draw conclusions.

Directions

1. Tightly wrap two pieces of aluminum foil all around the outside of the small jar. Be sure the dull sides of the foil are showing.
2. Carefully pour warm water into the small jar until it is almost full and immediately close it with the top. Then pour some warm water into the small glass until it is also almost full.
3. Position the cork inside the bottom of the large jar. Use the cork as a stand on which to place the small jar. Once the small jar is in position, tightly close the top of the large jar.
4. Wait for ten minutes.
5. Open the large jar and take out the small jar. Then open the small jar.
6. Test the temperature of the water in the small jar. Then test the temperature of the water in the small glass.

What did you think would happen before you did the experiment?

_____

_____

What happened during the experiment?

_____

_____

What can you conclude from the experiment?

_____

_____

Make a Compass

Matthew Henson might have been surprised to find out that his compass would not work at the North Pole. This is because the Earth's own magnetic field demagnetizes a compass, rendering it useless. That is why you are always told to keep magnets far away from a compass. However, did you know that you could use a magnet to make a compass? Use this activity to find out how to make a compass using a magnet.

Materials

- a 1 in. x 1 in. (2.54 cm x 2.54 cm) piece of sponge
- a thimble that is used for sewing
- tapestry needle (A sewing needle may be substituted, but special care must be taken so as not to stick yourself or someone else.)
- a bar magnet
- a small bowl
- water
- liquid detergent
- plastic spoon

Directions

1. Hold the eye of the needle while you stroke the point of the needle 20–30 times over one pole, or end, of the bar magnet. Be sure to make all of your strokes go in the same direction and use only one pole of the magnet.

2. Try to use the needle to pick up the paper clip. If it picks up the paper clip, the needle is magnetized. If it does not pick up the paper clip, continue to rub the needle against the magnet. Be sure you are correctly following the directions in Step 1. After your needle is magnetized, remove the bar magnet from your work area.

3. Squeeze the sponge so that it bends in half. Then carefully stick the needle through the bend of the sponge.

4. Put two drops of detergent into the bowl; fill it halfway with water. Then stir.

5. Carefully place the sponge with the needle in it on top of the water.

6. Gently spin the sponge and observe what happens.

What happened to the needle?

_____

_____

In which direction do you think the needle was pointing?

_____

_____

What would happen if you put the magnet next to the needle? Try it and find out.

_____

_____

Venn Diagram

You can use a Venn diagram to improve your comprehension of the stories you have read in this unit. Use the diagram shown below to compare and contrast two people, places, things, or events. For example, you could write Blanche at the top of one circle and Rose at the top of the other circle. The traits that are unique to each character are written where the two circles are independent of each other, under the appropriate name. The traits that are shared by the two characters are written where the two circles overlap, under the word Both.

Example:

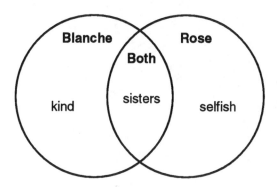

Suggested topics to compare and contrast using a Venn diagram include: Blanche/Rose, Blanche and Rose's Mother/The Old Woman, *The Talking Eggs/Roll of Thunder, Hear My Cry,* Cassie/Lillian Jean, Stacey/T.J., Great Faith School/Jefferson Davis School, Mr. Logan/Mr. Morrison, *Roll of Thunder, Hear My Cry/One More River to Cross,* Fannie Lou Hamer/Malcolm X, and Marian Anderson/Romare Bearden.

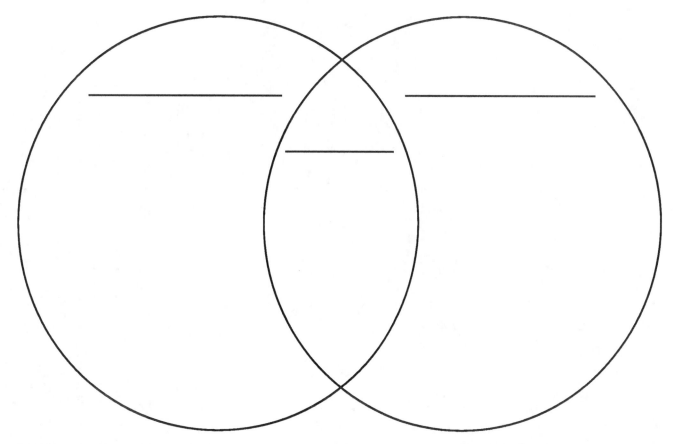

Comparing Maps

You can learn many things about Africa by comparing a climate map and a population map. Study the maps below. Then, on separate paper, answer the questions that appear at the bottom of the page.

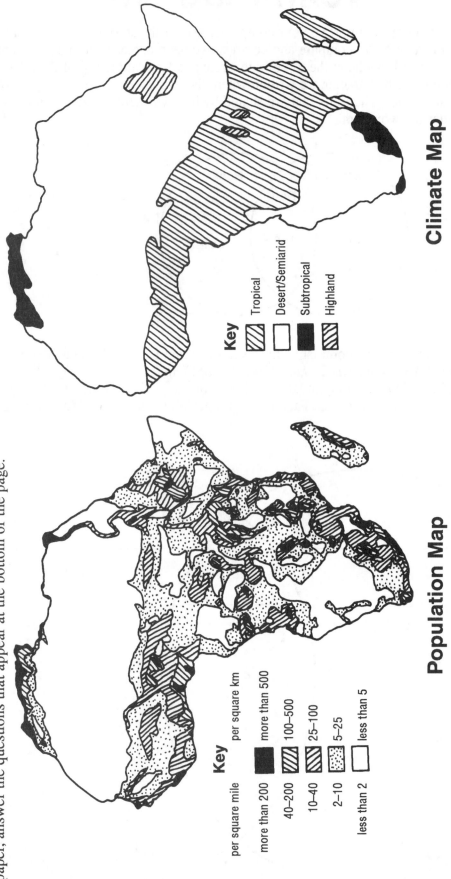

Climate Map

Key
- Tropical
- Desert/Semiarid
- Subtropical
- Highland

Population Map

Key

per square mile | per square km
- more than 200 | more than 500
- 40–200 | 100–500
- 10–40 | 25–100
- 2–10 | 5–25
- less than 2 | less than 5

1. How many climate zones are shown on the climate map?
2. What is the climate line in the area where there are the fewest people?
3. Where do most of the people live in northern Africa?
4. What is the population range for the subtropical areas of southern Africa?
5. Why do you think more people live in the area with a highland climate than the surrounding land?
6. What is the climate like where most people live in western Africa?
7. Pretend that you are moving to Africa. In which part of the continent would you choose to live? Explain your answer.

Concentration

This game increases your students' awareness of the important contributions made by individuals throughout history. Students play Concentration by matching the picture and name of a famous African American with his or her biographical sketch.

Directions

1. Provide students with copies of pages 62–65. Read over the biographical information with students. If you would like students to make cards of their own, provide copies of the blank cards at the bottom of this page.

2. Have students glue the cards onto one color of construction paper or tagboard and cut them out. Now each student should have a set of 24 playing cards, 12 portraits (pictures) with names, and 12 biographical sketches.

3. Have students pick partners. Ask them to place their cards face down and play Concentration.

4. A player scores a point each time a portrait is matched with a biographical sketch.

Students may use these blank cards to add more famous African Americans to this game.

Concentration Cards

Alice Walker
(1944-   )

In her younger years, she was very involved in the civil rights movement. She became a writer and teacher of literature at Jackson State College. She wrote mostly poetry. In 1970, she wrote her first novel, *The Third Life of Grange Copeland.* In the 1970's, she taught at Wellesley College and wrote many books and poems. In 1982, she wrote her most famous book, *The Color Purple.* This book won the Pultizer Prize, the American Book Award, and a National Book Critics Circle Award Nomination. Steven Spielberg then produced the story as a movie, and it received several Academy Award nominations.

Harriet Tubman
(1821?-1913)

This woman, who was an escaped slave herself, led as many as 300 people out of slavery in the South to freedom in the North. Despite the fact that there was a $40,000 reward for her capture, she returned to the South 19 times to help African Americans make the trip using the Underground Railroad. She was able to obtain freedom for her husband and elderly parents making this dangerous journey. She worked as a laundress, cook, and seamstress to pay for these trips. During the Civil War, she worked as a cook, nurse, scout, as well as a spy for the Union Army.

Wilma Rudolph
(1940-1994)

This woman made incredible achievements in athletics. She was born into a family of 22 children. At the age of four, she suffered scarlet fever and polio. This left her weak and partially crippled. The doctors said she probably would never walk again. She worked hard to prove that the doctors were wrong. She did learn to walk again and later found that she loved to run in track and field events. At the age of 16, she won the Bronze Medal in a relay at the 1956 Olympics. In the 1960 Olympics, she earned three gold medals in the races that she ran.

Concentration Cards *(cont.)*

Martin Luther King, Jr.
(1929-1968)

This man was one of the most important and influential leaders of the twentieth century. In 1955, he organized the famous Montgomery Bus Boycott. Throughout the 1950's and 1960's he worked for the civil rights of all people. He was strongly influenced by the words of Ghandi and stressed the use of nonviolent protest to cause change. In 1964, he received the Nobel Peace Prize. On April 4, 1968, he was assassinated by James Earl Ray. Today his birthday is celebrated as a federal holiday.

Oprah Winfrey
(1954-   )

This woman graduated from Tennessee State with a degree in speech and drama. She began working as a reporter and anchorperson in Chicago. She hosted a talk show in Chicago which was syndicated nationally in 1986. This was the first time an African-American woman had hosted her own national talk show. It is now the leading talk show in the country. She then created her own production company and named it Harpo Productions. In addition, she was Miss Black Tennessee in 1971 and was nominated for an Academy Award for her work in the film "The Color Purple."

Duke Ellington
(1899-1974)

He is known as the greatest of all jazz composers and musicians. He wrote his first song at the age of 17. He went on to introduce the human voice as an instrument, use echo chambers to create sound effects, add Cuban/Latin elements to jazz, and create the "jungle" sound. He played at the Cotton Club in Harlem from 1924–1927. He received a Grammy for his achievement in the music industry.

Concentration Cards *(cont.)*

Mary McLeod Bethune
(1875-1955)

This woman was a teacher and was strongly concerned with educational needs of African-American children. In 1904, with only $1.50, she created the Daytona Normal and Industrial School now called Bethune-Cookman College. She became the vice president of the National Urban League in 1920 and a member of the National Association of Colored Women from 1924–1928. She also began a hospital that treated African Americans.

Elijah McCoy
(1843-1929)

Although born in 1843, this man was never a slave. His inventions were primarily the lubricating parts of a steam engine. His parts were so far superior to all others that when customers bought these parts, they would ask if they were the "real McCoy." When he died, he had over 57 patents for inventions, such as the lawn sprinkler and the folding ironing board. However, he could not afford to finance the refining of his inventions. Consequently, those who paid for this work to be done made the huge profits off his inventions, and he died having made little money.

Ida Wells
(1862-1931)

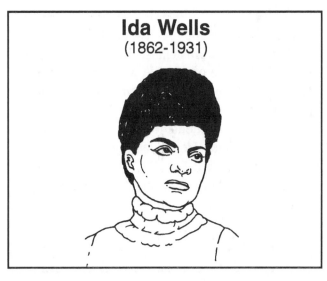

She began working as a teacher, but she was dismissed in 1891 because of her militant resistance to segregation. She is best known for her anti-lynching campaign. In 1892, she became half-owner of an African-American newspaper called The Memphis Free Speech. In this paper, she strongly criticized the lynching of African Americans. Her work was not limited to the anti-lynching campaign. She also organized the Black Women's Suffrage Organization, the National Afro-American Council, and the Committee of Forty which led to the development of the NAACP.

Concentration Cards *(cont.)*

Thurgood Marshall
(1908 -   )

This man was the first black justice of the United States Supreme Court. He started practicing law in 1933. From the late 1930s until 1961, he was chief counsel for the National Association for the Advancement of Colored People (NAACP). His legal arguments led to the 1954 Supreme Court decision making racial segregation unconstitutional in public schools.

Shirley Chisholm
(1924 -   )

She was the first African-American woman to become a member of the United States Congress. This woman was born in Brooklyn, New York. She graduated from Brooklyn College and moved on to Columbia University to earn her master's degree. Throughout her political career, this woman has worked toward reform in the legislature that would help more citizens. In addition to her valuable years of service in politics, she wrote an autobiography called *Unbought and Unbossed,* published in 1970.

Jesse Owens
(1913 - 1980)

This famous African American won four gold medals at the 1936 Olympic Games in Berlin. He was born in Oakville, Alabama, but later moved to Cleveland, Ohio. At Ohio State University, his athletic ability was recognized, when, in 1935, he broke three world records. In his career, this man set seven world records.

Kwanzaa

What is Kwanzaa?

Many cultures have special celebrations. In 1966, Dr. Maulana Karenga decided African Americans should have a celebration that would be uniquely theirs. He wanted this celebration to occur between December 26 and January 1 each year. He thought it would give African Americans a chance to learn about their African heritage, as well as plan for the future.

From where did the word Kwanzaa come?

In Africa, many tribes celebrate the first harvest of the crops. In Swahili this celebration is called Matunda ya Kwanza which means "First Fruits." Dr. Karenga used this name Kwanza to tie the new holiday to this tradition. However, he changed the name of the holiday to Kwanzaa by adding an extra "a." The purpose of this change in spelling was to show that the holiday was built on the old tradition, but also represented the beginning of a new tradition. The spelling now uses seven letters which indicate the number of days included in the holiday.

How is Kwanzaa celebrated?

There are special objects used for the Kwanzaa celebration. The first is mkeke (m-KEH-ka), which is a handmade mat. Next is a kikombe cha umoja (kee-KOM-beh chah oo-MO-jah) which is a cup that everyone drinks from to show that African Americans are a united people. One ear of corn, called muhindi (moo-HIN-de), is put out for each child in the family and is a reminder that children are the hope of the future. Next is the kinara (ki-NAH-rah), a wooden candleholder. It holds seven candles—one candle is black to symbolize African Americans, three candles are red to symbolize hard work and the fight for freedom, and three candles are green to symbolize hope. The last items on the table are gifts. They are called zawadi (zah-WAH-dee) and are handmade.

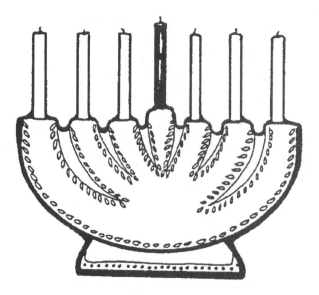

Each night for seven nights the family gets together, and one candle is lit as someone explains the belief for that day. On the first night, the black candle is lit to celebrate umoja (oo-MOE-jah), which means unity. On the second night, a red candle is lit for kujichagulia (koo-jee-cha-goo-LEE-ah), which means self-determination. On the third night, a green candle is lit for ujima (oo-JEE-mah), which means collective work and responsibility. On the fourth night, a red candle is lit for ujama (oo-jah-MAAH), cooperative economics. On the fifth night, a green candle is lit for nia (NEE-ah), which means purpose. On the sixth night, a candle is lit for kuumba (ku-OOM-bah, which means creativity. It is on the sixth night that the family has a huge feast. However, the last night is thought to be the best. All the candles are finally lit, and the belief is imani (ee-MAHN-ee), which means that good will always happen. After the candles are lit, everyone exchanges their zawadi, or gifts.

Kwanzaa Activities

Use the following activities as you learn about the Kwanzaa celebration (page 66) or as part of your cultures day (page 72) activities and displays.

Mkeka

In Africa, a mkeka would be made from straw and woven by hand. In this activity, you will make a paper mkeka.

Materials: 18" x 12" (46 cm x 30 cm) pieces of construction paper (one red, one green, one black), scissors, glue

Directions

1. Cut four strips of paper that are 18 inches (46 cm) long and 1 inch (2.54 cm) wide from each of the three colors of construction paper (red, green, and black). You should have a total of 12 strips.

2. On a flat surface, place the strips next to each other so they look like vertical lines with alternating colors. Be sure the ends of the strips are aligned.

3. Cut six strips of paper that are 12 inches (30 cm) long and 1 inch (2.54 cm) wide from each of the different colors of construction paper (red, green and black). You should have a total of 18 strips.

4. Glue one 12 inch (30 cm) strip along the top edge of the 18 inch (46 cm) strips. Allow the glue to dry. This will help you hold the long strips together as you weave in additional strips.

5. Starting next to the 12 inch (30 cm) strip you glued, weave in each of the other 12 inch (30 cm) strips. Weaving means you go above and below alternating strips of paper and continue with that pattern until you reach the end.

6. Secure the ends of the strips that you have woven by gluing them to the long strips.

Kinara

No Kwanzaa celebration would be complete without a kinara. Here is how you can make one to display at school.

Materials: a wooden board about 12" x 3" x 1" (30 cm x 8 cm x 2.54 cm), seven bottle caps from 2 or 3 liter bottles, modeling clay, 1 black dinner candle, 3 red dinner candles, 3 green dinner candles

Directions

1. Cover the top of the board with a layer of clay. You may wish to use different colored clay, make designs, or use a variety of tools to add texture.

2. Press each bottle cap into the clay on the board until all seven are in a row.

3. Mold additional clay around the outside of the bottle caps. Be sure you use plenty of clay to secure the bottle caps to the board, since this will be the stand for your candles.

4. Carefully place the candles into the stand in the following order: black candle in the middle, 3 red candles to the left of the black candle, and 3 green candles to the right of the black candle.

5. Use additional clay to connect the candles to the bottle caps. Be sure the candles cannot fall over or shift position.

6. Display your kinara at school. Then take it home and tell your family about it. Have an adult in your family light the kinara so everyone can enjoy it.

Story Filmstrips

You can have students make their own filmstrips to tell a story. Begin by collecting old filmstrips from libraries or other community resources. Place a bucket of undiluted bleach in a safe place away from students. Soak the old filmstrips in the bleach until they are completely clean. Wear rubber dishwashing gloves to remove the filmstrips from the bleach. Then rinse the filmstrips with clean water. Allow them to dry thoroughly before providing them to students.

In this activity students will use their written and oral language, sequencing skills, and artistic talents to create unique story filmstrips. This project can be done by individuals, partners, or cooperative learning groups.

Provide the following directions for students:

1. Have students pick a topic for their story. Have students brainstorm a list of possible topics that are related to this unit, or use the ideas suggested at the bottom of this page.

2. Have students decide which major events they will show on their filmstrip. Have them use a sentence strip to sketch their plan. Remind students that they must tell their entire story on a very limited amount of space.

3. Have students use fine-point permanent markers to make a title screen, a credits screen, and the story frames. If the filmstrip story is based on a reading selection, have students be sure to give the title and author of the book on the credits screen. For example students could show that a story filmstrip was "Adapted from *The Talking Eggs* by Robert D. San Souci."

4. Allow students to preview their filmstrip and make changes if necessary. Have students prepare a script of the story that goes with the filmstrip. Students may wish to read the script while showing the filmstrip, or they can record it on a tape and play the tape while showing the filmstrip.

5. Invite students to share their filmstrip story with the class.

Suggested Topics for Filmstrips

Have students use story filmstrips to…

- give a book report about *The Talking Eggs* or *Roll of Thunder, Hear My Cry*.
- create a story about Blanche's adventures in the city.
- make a series about different folk tales.
- tell about Cassie's life as an adult.
- tell T.J.'s story about breaking into the mercantile store.
- tell about other historical fiction stories that are related to African Americans.
- advertise the book *One More River to Cross*.
- make a series of biographies about famous African Americans.
- tell how African Americans have contributed to your state's history.

Present a Puppet Show

In this activity, you will make the fictional characters or real-life heroes you have read about in this unit come alive through puppetry. Work with three or four other students to pick a scene or event that you would like to present as a puppet show. Write a script for your puppet show. Then make a puppet to represent each of the characters or heroes.

Here is what you will need to make each puppet.

- a sock
- cotton balls or tissue
- different colors of yarn
- a variety of materials such as fabrics, buttons, bows, felt, permanent marker, etc.
- glue

Directions for Making a Sock Puppet

1. Use cotton balls or tissue to stuff the end of the sock to make the head.

2. Loosely tie a piece of yarn below the stuffing to make the neck. You will need to be able to get one finger through the neck and into the head.

3. Put your index finger into the puppet's head. Then on each side of the sock cut a small hole, one for your thumb and the other for the finger next to your index finger. Your thumb and finger will be the puppet's arms.

4. Use yarn for the hair and other materials to make the hero's face and clothing.

Present a Skit

A very effective way to experience what you read is to present a skit of a scene or event from the book. Work with three or four other students to pick a scene or event that you would like to present as a skit. Use the following organizer to help plan your skit.

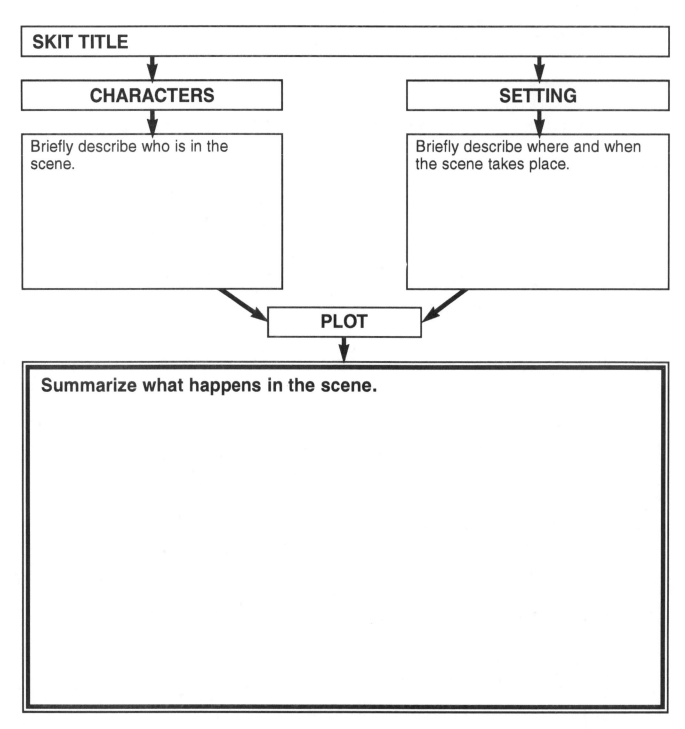

SKIT TITLE

CHARACTERS

Briefly describe who is in the scene.

SETTING

Briefly describe where and when the scene takes place.

PLOT

Summarize what happens in the scene.

As you work together to write your skit, you may want to include the use of a few special props or some simple scenery. After the skit is written, rehearse it several times. Practice speaking loudly and clearly so the audience will be able to understand you. When all in your group feel comfortable performing their parts, present your skit to the class.

African Recipes

What kind of food do you like to eat? Have you ever wondered where the recipes for those foods originated? You might be surprised to find that many of the foods you eat come from different places around the world. You can learn some interesting things about a culture by studying their recipes. In this activity, you will prepare some foods that come from different countries in Africa.

As you make these recipes, always work under the supervision of an adult and follow all kitchen safety rules.

Stew from Zaire

Ingredients

- 2 onions
- ¼ cup (60 mL) oil (vegetable or peanut)
- 1 chicken, cut into pieces
- 1 tomato
- 1 teaspoon (5 mL) salt
- ½ teaspoon (2.5 mL) pepper
- 1 cup (250 mL) water
- 2 cups (500 mL) tomato juice
- cayenne pepper (optional)

Directions

1. Take the skin off the onion and dice into small pieces.
2. Use paper towels to wipe off any excess moisture on the pieces of chicken.
3. Place the oil in a pot and heat on medium for one minute.
4. Put the chicken and the onions into the oil and brown them. Use a spatula to keep turning the mixture over. Once the mixture is brown, remove it from the pot and put it on a plate.
5. Pour out the oil. Then place the chicken and onion mixture back into the pot with two tablespoons (30 mL) of oil.
6. Slice the tomato into sections and add them to the pot. Mix in the salt, pepper, water, and tomato juice.
7. Cook for 45 minutes over a low heat.
8. Make a gravy for the stew by stirring 3 tablespoons (45 mL) of flour into 3 tablespoons (45 mL) of hot water. After the gravy has thickened, pour it over the chicken.

Groundnut Soup from Nigeria

Ingredients

- 1 tomato (large)
- 1 potato (large)
- 1 onion (medium)
- 2 cups (500 mL) water
- 1 beef bouillon cube
- 1 teaspoon (5 mL) salt
- 1 cup (250 mL) finely chopped peanuts (shelled, unsalted, roasted)
- ½ cup (125 mL) of peanut butter may be substituted for the peanuts
- ½ cup (125 mL) milk
- 2 tablespoons (30 mL) rice

Directions

1. Remove the peel from the onion and the potato.
2. Use a knife to cut the potato, tomato, and onion into tiny pieces.
3. In a pan, combine the potato, tomato, onion, water, bouillon cube, and salt. Place the lid on the pan and gently boil for 30 minutes.
4. In a bowl, mix the peanuts or peanut butter with the milk until smooth.
5. Pour the rice and the peanut mixture into the pan with the other ingredients.
6. Use a spoon to mix the soup. Cook over low heat for at least 30 minutes.

Cultures Day

Divide the class into cooperative learning groups and have a Cultures Day. Have students brainstorm to make a list of activities they could use to tell other students about different cultures, or use the suggestions that are provided below. Then have students make the necessary preparations for the Cultures Day. Finally, have students invite other classes to participate in this event.

Invitations: Have students make invitations to ask other classes to come to this special event. Have them make advertisements to display in the hallway that will make teachers and students want to attend.

Big Books: Have students make a big book that tells a story that comes from a particular culture. Punch three holes on the left-hand side of six pieces of poster board. Have students each use one piece of poster board to create covers for their big books. Then have them use the rest of the poster board to illustrate five events from the story and write a short summary of each event. Ask students to put the pieces of poster board in order according to the events in the story. After the pieces of poster board are in order, have students connect the pages with metal rings or yarn. Allow students to use their big books to retell the story to younger children.

Guest Speakers: Invite people from the community to come and speak to students about different cultures and what makes each special. Encourage the guests to tell about their personal experiences and share any photographs or objects that provide students with the opportunity to get a real-life view and a better understanding of the things that are important to different culture groups.

Posters: Have students design posters to display around the school that promote world peace and cooperation among the peoples of the world.

Murals: Have students plan and draw murals (page 74) that show some of the important contributions that people from different cultures have made throughout history.

Heritage Quilts: Have students create heritage quilts (page 73) that tell about people from different cultures, such as the African Americans that were studied in this unit.

Recipes: Have students locate and make recipes from different cultures. Family members and local restaurants may be valuable resources for recipes. Be sure to use the African recipes shown in this unit (page 71).

An American Hero Scrapbook: Have the class work together on an American Hero Scrapbook. Have students include articles about and pictures of heroic people from different cultures.

Research Center: Set up the research center (page 76) found in this unit. Have students display the reports that they have written, using the research center. Be sure a variety of cultures is represented.

In addition to these activities, have students present skits (page 70) and puppet shows (page 69) as part of their Cultures Day activities.

Heritage Quilt

In this culminating activity, you will work with two or three other students to make a heritage quilt that tells about the different African Americans you have studied in this unit. You can make additional heritage quilts as you study other cultures.

Here is what you will need to make a heritage quilt.

• two sheets of butcher paper—each sheet, 2 feet x 2 feet (61 cm x 61 cm)

• 16 construction paper squares—each square, 6 inches x 6 inches (15 cm x 15 cm)

• colorful scraps or pieces of construction paper

• glue

Here are the directions for making your heritage quilt.

1. Pick 16 African Americans that you want to tell about on your quilt. On each quilt square, you will draw a picture of an African American and write a short biographical summary that includes a description of his or her contribution. Use the space below to plan what your quilt will look like.

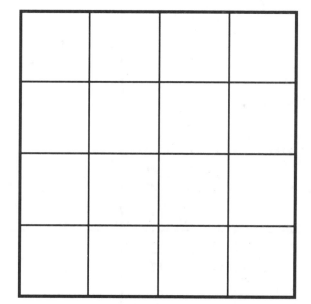

2. Glue the two sheets of butcher paper together. This will make the back of your quilt and the middle layer, which is called the interlining. Allow the glue to dry.

3. Decorate each construction paper square by drawing a picture of an African American and writing a brief description of that person's contribution.

4. Lay your squares on the interlining according to the plan you made above. Glue the squares down onto the interlining. Allow the glue to dry.

5. Display your heritage quilt on a wall or bulletin board.

Mural

Work with three or four other students to create a mural that shows any one of the following:

- scenes from four story events in *The Talking Eggs* or *Roll of Thunder, Hear My Cry*
- four important events from one African American's story as described in *One More River to Cross*
- one important event from four African Americans' stories as described in *One More River to Cross*

First, decide which four events you would like to show. Second, use the space below to plan what you will draw for each of these events. Third, paint the mural on a long piece of butcher paper or on four pieces of poster board that have been joined together with masking tape. Allow the mural to dry. Finally, display your mural for other students to enjoy.

Bulletin Boards

Working Together

Cover the background of the bulletin board with butcher paper. Draw a large balance scale in the middle. At the top of the board, display the title "Working Together." Then write the following terms on sentence strips, one set for each group: civil liberties, coexist, cooperation, desegregation, egalitarianism, Equal Rights Amendment, equality, ethical, impartial, integration, interdependence, justice, mutual respect, tolerance. Discuss the meanings of the terms. Then have students work together to divide the words into two groups so that there is an equal number of terms and an equal number of letters in each group. Ask groups to share their solutions. Finally, display one set of answers on the scale.

Kwanzaa

Make a bulletin board of the seven principles of Kwanzaa. For more information about Kwanzaa and activities related to this holiday, refer to *Kwanzaa Activities* (# 784—Teacher Created Materials, Inc., 1994).

Famous African Americans

Cover the background of the bulletin board with butcher paper, art tissue paper, or fabric. Have students do research about famous African Americans. Ask them to draw a portrait and write a report to display on the bulletin board. You can also use this bulletin board idea when studying your state history. Simply place a map of your state in the center of the bulletin board and have students do research for reports on African Americans who have made contributions in your state. Use the title "African Americans in (the name of your state)."

Folk Tales from Around the World

Cover the background of a bulletin board with butcher paper, wrapping paper, or aluminum foil. Place a world map in the middle with the title "Folk Tales from Around the World" above it. After students have completed the Folk Tale Comparison Chart (page 10), display them on the bulletin board.

Research Center

This research center is easy to make and will help motivate your students to learn about the different culture groups in America. Begin by cutting a large box so that you have three panels as shown in the diagram below. Poster board can be taped together to make the three panels, but it will not be as sturdy or stable as a box.

The Center Panel

Draw or cut out a picture of a large pot that might be used for melting metals. Place the words "The Melting Pot" on the front of the pot. Cut out the continents from a world map. Glue or staple the continents onto the center panel so that it looks as if they are falling into the pot.

The Left Panel

Make the title "Who's Who in Our Class." Cut index cards so that you have one-half a card for every student. Have students write their names and their cultural backgrounds on the half cards. If students do not know their cultural backgrounds, have them find out this information for homework. Glue or staple photographs of your students onto the panel. Below each photograph, glue the index card with that student's information. Discuss the different cultures that are represented in your class.

The Right Panel

Make the title "How to Do a Research Paper" on the right panel. Below the title, show the following steps:

Step 1: Locate sources of information.
Step 2: Read and take notes from the sources you have located.
Step 3: Make an outline to organize your notes.
Step 4: Use your outline to write your rough draft.
Step 5: Edit, proof, and correct your rough draft.
Step 6: Write your final draft.
Step 7: Ask a friend to read your final draft. Make any corrections and redo your final draft, if necessary.

Some Research Suggestions

African Americans:
Mary McLeod Bethune (educator), Frederick A. Douglass (abolitionist), Edward Brooke (senator), Leontyne Price (opera singer), Jackie Robinson (baseball player), Elijah McCoy (inventor), Gwendolyn M. Carter (scientist), Rosa Parks (civil rights leader)

Asian Americans:
Kristi Yamaguchi (skater), Ruth Wong (physician), Sadao S. Munemori (soldier), Daniel K. Inouye (senator), Wilfred Tsukiyama (Chief Justice), Patsy Mink (lawyer/legislator), Seong Moy (artist), James Wong Howe (cameraman for motion pictures)

Hispanic Americans:
Cesar Chavez (labor leader), Joan Baez (singer), Alfredo Hernandez (judge), Dolores Huerta (labor leader), Joseph Montoya (senator), Loreta Velazquez (soldier), Roberto Clemente (baseball player), Franklin Chang-Diaz (astronaut)

Native Americans:
Sacajawea (guide), Chief Joseph (leader), Osceola (leader), Pocahontas (princess), Quanah (leader), Jim Thorpe (football player), Tecumseh (leader), John Ross (leader)

Bibliography

Nonfiction

Adler. M. *The Paideia Program: An Educational Syllabus.* Macmillan, 1992.

Altman, Susan R. *Extraordinary Black Americans from Colonial to Contemporary Time.* Childrens Press, 1988.

Conrad, David E. *The Forgotten Farmers: The Story of Sharecroppers in the New Deal.* Greenwood, 1965.

Daniel, Becky. *Portraits in Black.* Good Apple, 1990.

Davis, Burke. *Black Heroes of the American Revolution.* HBJ, 1976.

Haber, Louis. *Black Pioneers of Science and Invention.* Harcourt, 1970.

Hancock, Sibyl. *Famous Firsts of Black Americans.* Pelican, 1983.

Haskins, James. *Black Dance in America.* HarperCollins, 1990.

Katz, William L. *Black People Who Made the Old West.* HarperCollins, 1989.

Lester, Julius, ed. *To Be a Slave.* Dial, 1968.

Levine, Ellen. *Freedom's Children: Young Civil Rights Activists Tell Their Own Stories.* Putman, 1993.

Miller, Robert. *Soldiers.* Silver Burdett Press, 1991.

Musgrove, Margaret. *Ashanti to Zulu: African Traditions.* Dial, 1976.

Myers, Walter Dean. *Now Is Your Time!: The African-American Struggle for Freedom.* Harper, 1991.

Richardson, Ben & Foley, William A. *Great Black Americans.* HarperCollins, 1990.

Ryan, Elizabeth. *Straight Talk about Prejudice.* Facts on File, 1992.

Sammons, Vivian O. *Blacks in Science and Medicine.* Hemisphere Publications, 1989.

Taylor, Roy G. *Sharecroppers: The Way We Really Were.* J Mark, 1984.

Biography

Adler, David A. *Martin Luther King, Jr.: Free at Last.* Holiday, 1986.

Collier, James Lincoln. *Louis Armstrong: An American Success Story.* Macmillan, 1985.

Ferris, Jeri. *Arctic Explorer: The Story of Matthew Henson.* Carolrhoda, 1989.

Ferris, Jeri. *Go Free or Die: A Story about Harriet Tubman.* Chelsea House, 1988.

Ferris, Jeri. *Walking the Road to Freedom: A Story about Sojourner Truth.* Carolrhoda, 1988.

Ferris, Jeri. *What Are You Figuring Now?: A Story about Benjamin Banneker.* Carolrhoda, 1988.

Greene, Carol. *Jackie Robinson: Baseball's First Black Major Leaguer.* Childrens, 1990.

Hamilton, Virginia. *Anthony Burns: The Defeat and Triumph of a Fugitive Slave.* Knopf, 1988.

Knapp, Ron. *Sports Great Isiah Thomas.* Enslow, 1992.

Lipsyte, Robert. *Free to Be Muhammad Ali.* Harper, 1978.

McKissack, Pat. *Jesse Jackson: A Biography.* Scholastic, 1989.

McKissack, Pat. *Jesse Owens: Olympic Star.* Enslow, 1992.

McKissack, Pat. *Langston Hughes: Great American Poet.* Enslow, 1992.

McKissack, Pat. *Madam C.J. Walker: Self-made Millionaire.* Enslow, 1992.

McKissack, Pat. *Ralph J. Bunche: Peacemaker.* Enslow, 1991.

McKissack, Pat. *The Story of Booker T. Washington.* Childrens Press, 1991.

Mitchell, Barbara. *Raggin', A Story about Scott Joplin.* Carolrhoda, 1987.

Myers, Walter Dean. *Malcolm X: By Any Means Necessary.* Scribner, 1993.

Naden, Corinne J. *Colin Powell: Straight to the Top.* Millbrook, 1991.

Patrick, Diane. *Coretta Scott King.* Watts, 1991.

Russell, Sharman. *Frederick Douglass.* Chelsea House, 1988.

Warner, Lucille Schulberg. *From Slave to Abolitionist: The Life of William Wells Brown.* Dial, 1993.

Wolfe, Rinna. *Charles Richard Drew, M.D.* Troll Associates, 1986.

Woods, Harold. *Bill Cosby: Making America Laugh and Learn.* Dillon, 1983.

Bibliography (cont.)

Fiction

Armstrong, William H. *Sounder.* Harper, 1969.

Armstrong, William H. *Sour Land.* Harper, 1971.

Fox, Paula. *Slave Dancer.* Bradbury, 1973.

Hamilton, Virginia. *Cousins.* Philomel, 1990.

Hamilton, Virginia. *The House of Dies Drear.* Macmillan, 1968.

Hamilton, Virginia. *The Mystery of Drear House.* Greenwillow Books, 1987.

Lester, Julius. *Long Journey Home: Stories from Black History.* Dial, 1972.

Lyons, Mary. *Letters from a Slave Girl: The Story of Harriet Jacobs.* Scribners, 1992.

McKissack, Pat. *The Dark-thirty: Southern Tales of the Supernatural.* Knopf, 1992.

Taylor, Mildred. *The Friendship.* Dial Books, 1987.

Taylor, Mildred. *The Gold Cadillac.* Dial Books, 1987.

Taylor, Mildred. *Let the Circle Be Unbroken.* Dial, 1981.

Taylor, Mildred. *Mississippi Bridge.* Dial, 1990.

Taylor, Mildred. *The Road to Memphis.* Dial, 1990.

Taylor, Mildred. *Song of the Trees.* Dial, 1975.

Turner, Ann Warren. *Nettie's Trip South.* MacMillan, 1987.

Wisler, G. Clifton. *The Raid.* Dutton, 1985.

Yates, Elizabeth. *Amos Fortune, Free Man.* Penguin, 1989.

Yep, Laurence. *Dragonwings.* Harper, 1975.

Folk Tales

Faison, Edward, Jr. *African American Folk Tales.* Vantage, 1989.

Gray, Stephen, ed. *The Penguin Book of Southern African Stories.* Viking Penguin, 1986.

Grifalconi, Ann. *The Village of the Round and Square Houses.* Little, 1986.

Hamilton, Virginia. *The People Could Fly.* Knopf, 1987.

Jones, Bessie & Hawes, Bess L. *Step It Down: Games, Plays, Songs, & Stories from the Afro-American Heritage.* University of Georgia Press, 1987.

Kipling, Rudyard. *Just So Stories.* HarperCollins, 1991.

Lester, Julius. *Black Folktales.* Grove Weidenfeld, 1991.

Lester, Julius. *Tales of Uncle Remus.* Dial, 1987.

Lester, Julius. *More Tales of Uncle Remus.* Dial, 1988.

Moore, Mary S. *Fireside Tales.* New Day Press, 1990.

Omoleye, Amoke. *Yoruba Children's Tales.* Amoke Omoleye Publications, 1990.

Parks, Van Dyke. *Jump!: The Adventures of Brer Rabbit.* Harcourt, 1986.

Parks, Van Dyke. *Jump Again!: More Adventures of Brer Rabbit.* Harcourt, 1987.

Pitcher, Diana. *Tokoloshi: African Folk Tales Retold.* Celestial Arts, 1990.

Pruett, Jakie L. & Cole, Everett B. *As We Lived—Stories Told by Black Story Tellers.* Eakin Press, 1982.

Teacher Created Materials

230   *Multicultural Folk Tales*

372   *Multicultural Bibliography*

439   *Literature Unit: Roll of Thunder, Hear My Cry*

530   *Literature Unit: Sounder*

615   *Multicultural Holidays*

617   *Multicultural Art Activities*

650   *Cooperative Learning Activities: Language Arts*

653   *Cooperative Learning Activities: Social Studies*

784   *Kwanzaa Activities*

Answer Key

Page 8

1. A long time..., 2. The widow made..., 3. Blanche ran away..., 4. Blanche saw many..., 5. Blanche scooped up..., 6. Valuable things..., 7. Rose went..., 8. Rose laughed..., 9. Rose took the old woman's..., 10. Rose took the jeweled..., 11. Horrible creatures..., 12. Blanche went...

Page 10

Author and Title: *The Talking Eggs* by Robert D. San Souci

Culture of Origin: Creole

Setting: the cabin that belonged to Blanche's family, the woods, the old woman's cabin

Characters and Character Traits: Rose—greedy, lazy, cruel, rude; Blanche—kind, thoughtful, hard-working; faithful to her word; helpful; The widowed mother—always angry, unfair, lazy, cruel, greedy; The old woman—unusual, caring, sincere, kind-hearted, appreciative, wise

Problem: Rose and the mother are cruel to Blanche. Blanche runs away from home. When Blanche returns home with treasures, greedy Rose tries to get some for herself. Rose tries to get a treasure, too. However, she makes all the wrong choices because she is greedy. As a result, she is chased by a pack of wild creatures.

Solution to Problem: Blanche always makes the right choice and is rewarded with eggs that have treasures inside. Rose and the mother are chased by a pack of wild creatures because they have been cruel and greedy.

Purpose of Story: To teach the lesson that generosity and kindness will be rewarded and that cruelty and greediness with be punished

Page 13

Cause

2. The old woman at the well was thirsty and asked Blanche to get her a drink.
4. Blanche had run away from home and was crying in the woods.
6. Blanche put an old beef bone in the pot.
8. Blanche threw the plain eggs over her left shoulder.
10. Rose took the fancy eggs, even though they said, "Don't take me."

Effect

1. Rose did not have to do any work.
3. Blanche was yelled at and hit by Rose and the mother.
5. Blanche went to the old woman's cabin.
7. Blanche took only the plain eggs because they are the ones that said, "Take me."
9. Rose and the mother were going to steal Blanche's treasures after Rose got her own treasures from the old woman.

Page 23 (top)

1. the narrow, sun-splotched road
2. Big Ma, who was working in the fields
3. the school bus
4. how Cassie slid down a wooden pole that was used to mark the length of the cotton field
5. the school bus after it went off the road
6. T.J. constantly talking while riding in the back of the wagon
7. Cassie as she led Lillian Jean into the forest
8. the sweat dripping off of Mr. Morrison as he lifted Kaleb Wallace's truck

Page 26

Causes should include:

Little Man threw the book down because it was old and dirty and designated to be used by African Americans. Cassie believed that she understood why Little Man had thrown the book down and refused to take it.

The teacher got angry when Cassie spoke up for Little Man and when she questioned why only old worn-out textbooks were good enough for African Americans.

Cassie helped to sabotage the Jefferson Davis County School bus so that those students would have to walk just like African-American children.

Mr. Barnett served other people before he served Cassie, even though she was there before those people. Then he called her a "Little Nigger."

Cassie accidentally bumped into Lillian Jean on the sidewalk. She was forced to apologize again by Mr. Simms and Big Ma.

Cassie wanted to get back at Lillian Jean for having humiliated her in town. She lured Lillian Jean into the woods by saying there was something to see there.

Uncle Hammer came every winter to spend the Christmas season with Cassie's family.

R.W. and Melvin Simms had lied and said that two other African-American boys had been with T.J. when the mercantile was robbed.

T.J. was injured from having been beaten up by R.W. and Melvin. He stopped by to ask Cassie and Stacey for their help.

Cassie saw that African Americans were being discriminated against. Cassie was proud of who she was.

Answer Key *(cont.)*

Page 36
Suggested answers:

Red Blood Cells: called erythrocytes, constantly circulating in bloodstream, carry oxygen to tissues and lungs, carry out carbon dioxide, 4-6 million in microliter, mature cell has no nucleus, looks fat and doughnut shaped with a hole

White Blood Cells: called leukocytes, produced in bone marrow, provide protection from disease and infection, 4000-10,000 in a microliter, has a nucleus, three types—neutrophils, lymphocytes, and monocytes

Platelets: disk shaped; made from cells produced in bone marrow; allows blood to clot to stop bleeding; 150,000-400,000 in a microliter

Plasma: is a liquid, mostly water; contains proteins, foodstuffs, and clotting substances; is the color of straw; makes up 55-65% of the blood

Page 37
House of Representatives (top half): A bill is introduced; clerk reads it aloud; sent to committee.

Committee: Committee members study the bill; expert witnesses are asked to speak; can release bill, revise it, or table it; if released or revised and released, the bill goes back to the House.

House of Representatives (bottom half): Amendments are made; the bill must be approved by more than one-half the House (simple majority) to be passed on to the Senate.

Senate (top half): With the vice-president's permission, the bill is introduced by a senator; bill goes to a committee.

Committee: Committee members study the bill; the bill can be approved, revised, or tabled; if approved or revised and approved, the bill is sent back to the Senate.

Senate (bottom half): The bill is debated; it must be approved by more than one-half of the Senate (simple majority) before it is passed on to a conference committee.

Conference Committee: Made up of members from the House and the Senate; they work together to combine the version of the bill that was passed by the House and the version of the bill that was passed by the Senate; final version of bill must be approved by both the House and the Senate.

Speaker of the House: Signs the bill and gives it to the Vice-President.

Vice-President: Signs the bill, after which it is sent to the President.

President

Veto: Rejects the bill; sends the bill back to Congress with an explanation of why it was rejected.

No Action: Refuses to sign the bill; if Congress is in session and the bill is not signed within ten days, it becomes a law without the President's signature; if Congress adjourns the session before the ten day period is up, the bill cannot become a law without the President's signature.

Approved: If the President feels the bill will make a good law, he or she signs it, dates it, and writes "approved" on it.

Page 52
1. Harriet Tubman
2. Rosa Parks
3. James Armistead
4. Maya Angelou
5. Oprah Winfrey
6. Jesse Jackson
7. Martin Luther King, Jr.
8. Sojourner Truth
9. Booker T. Washington
10. Jackie Robinson

Page 54
Is It Magic?
1. Hypothesis: Answers will vary.
2. a. The egg sank. b. The egg floated.
3. The salt kept the egg afloat.

Testing Inertia
2. Hypothesis: Answers will vary.
3. The egg fell into the glass.
4. The egg has enough inertia to stand still, so it falls into the glass.

Page 55
Cooked or Raw?
1. Hypothesis: Answers will vary.
2. a. The cooked egg stopped spinning.; b. the raw egg continued to spin.
3. The liquid in the the raw egg continues to spin even if the egg is stopped momentarily. When the egg is released, it begins to spin again due to the motion of the liquid.

Egg in a Bottle
3. Hypothesis: Answers will vary.
6. The egg is pulled into the bottle.
7. The gases inside the bottle expand due to the heat. They are pushed out of the bottlle. When the heat source is gone the gases contract. This creates a vacuum, which combines with the outside air pressure to pull the egg into the bottle.

Page 58
The needle stops spinning.

It points to the north.

The needle is attracted to the magnet, so it will move in the direction of the magnet.